Polarity Coac

Coaching People and Managing Polarities

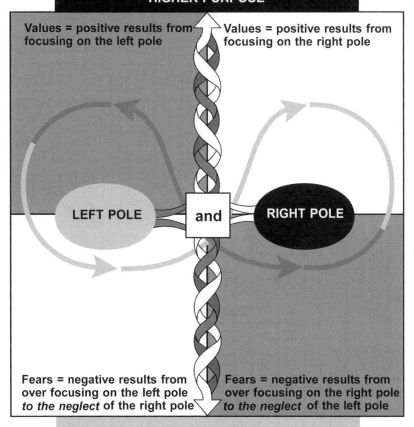

Kathy Anderson

HRD Press, Inc. • Amherst • Massachusetts

Published by: HRD Press, Inc.
22 Amherst Road
Amherst, MA 01002
413-253-3488
800-822-2801 (U.S. and Canada)
413-253-3490 (fax)
www.hrdpress.com

ISBN 978-1-59996-207-8

Editorial services by Sally M. Farnham
Production services by Jean Miller
Cover design by Eileen Klockars

To Bobby
The wind beneath my wings

Table of Contents

Acknowledgments

First and foremost I wish to thank Dr. Barry Johnson, founder and president of Polarity Management® Associates and author of *Polarity Management: Identifying and Managing Unsolvable Problems.* My husband and I were fortunate to have dinner with Barry and his wife, Dana, and while enjoying the conversation about my latest coach training experience, Barry looked at me and said, "There is a book to be written that blends polarity management and coaching." Those words inspired and framed the vision for *Polarity Coaching*™. Thank you, Barry, for Polarity Management®, the body of work you founded; for all you have so generously shared; and for your mission of "Enhancing our quality of life on the planet by supplementing the way we think."

Many thanks to the Polarity Management® learning community for your encouragement and I am very grateful to all who read drafts and gave me incredibly valuable feedback and to family and friends for their encouragement.

Thank you to all who have shared their coaching stories with me. These stories helped shape the coaching cases for this book, and I am incredibly grateful!

And finally, I wish to thank Margaret Seidler, who so skillfully coached me using a Polarity Map™, oh so many years ago.

Foreword

In *Coaching People and Managing Polarities*, Kathy Anderson has done a masterful job of providing a new, supplemental approach for coaches. Kathy skillfully brings together Polarity Management® and Coaching principles to create Polarity Coaching™. Polarity Coaching answers the question, "What do I do when I am coaching someone who is trying to solve a difficulty that is inherently unsolvable and unavoidable?" In this book of seven case studies, Kathy uses fundamental polarities in coaching and shows how to distinguish between problems that can be solved and polarities that need to be managed. When those we are coaching can see and manage polarities, they can tap them as a resource for enhancing their lives.

In the last fifty years, there has been a growing interest in the power of polarities. Being able to apply Polarity Management to coaching helps clients see the whole picture and the natural pattern that is at play in so many of our life experiences. As you read the cases, you will see how Polarity Coaching enriches the conversation as the client unveils the dynamic balance within a polarity. Kathy introduces the Polarity Map™ and layers Polarity Management principles together with coaching techniques to create, with the client, a visual structure that works. The Polarity Map and principles are a wisdom organizer, and the wisdom is in the life experience of the client.

Coaching People and Managing Polarities is both a gift to coaches and to the people they coach. It is my pleasure to recommend this book to anyone wanting to build their professional coaching skills and broaden their coaching practice to include Polarity Coaching.

Barry Johnson,
Founder of Polarity Management

Introduction

This book brings together the art and skill of coaching with the science and form of Polarity Management®. It is about coaching people, managing polarities, and the blending of the two disciplines, that opens an opportunity to see and experience predictive patterns that would not otherwise be visible. This is what I call Polarity Coaching™.

Coaching people emerged as a profession in the 1990s, and today coaching is a recognized discipline used by professional coaches to engage people in their development. Whitworth, et al. (1998)[1] stated that "The coach's job is to help clients articulate their dreams, desires and aspirations, help them clarify their mission, purpose and goals, and help them achieve that outcome" (p. 5). Each coach training program I have attended and every coaching book I have read echo this.

This book, *Polarity Coaching: Coaching People and Managing Polarities*, is dedicated to building on that concept through the blending of Coaching and Polarity Management. This book is about Polarity Coaching™. The Polarity Map™, a supplement to traditional coaching methods, will enhance your effectiveness as a coach and create a stretch for your client. Polarity Coaching uses the same powerful questions and visioning of traditional coaching; in addition, it provides a structure for the client to walk through his or her story in a collective fashion that will uncover values and fears, as well as develop action steps and early warnings.

How many times have you coached someone who has a great vision and is committed to the goal and action steps that will get him or her there, however, the client simply fails to fully walk the vision or reach the goal? Or perhaps the client met his or her goal, but then wasn't able to sustain it and ultimately fell back into old, more familiar patterns. This often happens because the coach and the client are only looking at half the picture; they are only looking at one component of the goal or the vision—one pole or motivational value—and they are unable to see the interdependent pole, also called the interdependent value. The client may really want to make and sustain change, and the coach may want to continue to coach in traditional ways by asking the right questions and supporting, encouraging, and working with the client, but this may not really be helping the client make progress.

---

[1] *Co-Active Coaching: New Skills for Coaching People Toward Success in Work and Life.* Davies–Black Publishing, Boston: MA.

Understanding the client's goal and motivational values is key to the coaching experience, and, with Polarity Coaching, understanding the client's interdependent values provides powerful predictive insights for the client that is unique to the coaching experience. Using the visual map helps the coach and the client see the gaps and know where to explore. In addition, it provides a structure to use and to revisit as needed to focus on the vision or the goal and to hold the client accountable.

The cases in this book are based on classic polarities and demonstrate how Polarity Management complements and enhances the coaching experience. Naming the polarity, the interdependent pair, is the beginning of an expanded coaching conversation that is the "difference that makes a difference" in the coaching experience. Polarity Coaching creates a meta view of the client's goal or value from not one, but rather two perspectives and enables a more complete picture to emerge. With Polarity Coaching, the client's action plan becomes a set of action steps and early warnings, building a picture of predictive understanding of what will occur when he or she is living his or her values (or not), and develops a visible pattern that flows through the interdependent pairs.

I am confident that you will see from the following stories how Polarity Coaching can transform the coaching conversation and create a unique potential and powerful combination for coaching people and managing polarities.

> **Note:** Although these cases are based on data gathered during an interview process, names and situations have been modified.

Motivational Values

While attending my first coach training session in 2001, I learned about motivational values. Polarity Coaching is based on the principles of Polarity Management and the fact that we all have motivational values that drive our view of any given situation. In other words, our view of any given situation is typically driven from what is valued, a motivational value, or preferred pole. What is unknown, or what we are typically blind to, is our non-preferred pole, also known as the motivational value's interdependent pair. I use all these terms throughout the book, and I am sure that while reading the cases, these terms will become familiar and you will be able to use these terms interchangeably as I have.

Polarity Management® Principles

To help identify the components of the Polarity Map, I have placed inserts throughout the case narrative to identify each principle as it is introduced to the client. You will see them unfold in multiple ways, as there is no recommended way; whatever works best with your client is the best method.

Naming the Map: Client's ultimate vision

Greater Purpose Statement: What the client wants to achieve, the incentive, the reference point for the work

Deeper Fear: What to avoid, the disincentive

Naming the Polarity Poles (interdependent poles): Each pole should have a neutral name; refer to Appendix A for examples

Virtuous Cycle: Upward spiraling synergy arrows that lift the system and depict the potential for the tension between the two poles to positively reinforce one another toward the Greater Purpose Statement

Vicious Cycle: Downward spiraling synergy arrows that drop the system and depict the potential for the tension between the two poles to negatively reinforce one another toward the Deeper Fear

Infinity Loop: The dynamic flow of the Infinity Loop demonstrates how a polarity oscillates from one pole to the other over time; the goal being to experience a well-balanced flow and gain positive results from the upsides of both poles

Upper Left Quadrant: Positive results experienced when focusing on the preferred pole

Lower Left Quadrant: Negative results experienced when there is an over focus on the preferred pole to the neglect of the other, interdependent pole

Upper Right Quadrant: Positive results experienced when focusing on the interdependent pole

Lower Right Quadrant: Negative results experienced when there is an over focus on the interdependent pole to the neglect of the preferred pole

Early Warnings: A sign that too much focus has been given to a single pole and one must look to the action steps of the interdependent pole to regain balance; Early Warnings should be measurable

Action Steps: The steps needed to regain balance with the interdependent pole after experiencing one or more Early Warnings of the focused pole; action steps should be achievable

Where to Start

The cases in this book build from the simple to more complex. I have tried to demonstrate that there is no single starting point to explain or begin working the map. The coach simply starts where the client is, whether it's naming the poles, stating the Greater Purpose, focusing on a fear or concern, or identifying an important value. It is important, however, when working the quadrants to follow a natural order of thinking using the dynamic flow of the Infinity Loop starting with the upper left, to lower left, to upper right, and finally to lower right. The exception to this is when there is resistance to the value of the nonpreferred pole; you will see how this works in Case Study #4. It is also important to follow the Infinity Loop through Action Steps and Early Warnings, but the starting point for Action Steps and Early Warnings can vary depending on the client situation.

How to Use the Tool

Each case in this book steps through the coaching process using the Polarity Map in a slightly different way. This is done to demonstrate that the Polarity Map works in most any setting. Polarity Coaching can be used in a face-to-face coaching session writing on paper, white boards, or even easel paper and masking tape on the floor to create a Polarity Map that you can physically walk through while coaching your client. Polarity Coaching can easily be used during phone appointments, and maps can be drawn by client and coach alike during the coaching session or drawn by the coach and shared using e-mail attachments. There is no one recommended way—whatever works best with your client is the best method for Polarity Coaching.

Case Study #1
Work and Home

It is possible to manage a polarity well and gain positive results of both upsides while minimizing the negative effects of both downsides. However, over focusing on one pole, to the neglect of the other pole, will, over time, lead to the downside of the very pole on which you have over focused. There will be a lack of balance in your life, and eventually you will find yourself living out your deeper fear. That is what happened to Dan.

By any standard, Dan had a full and happy life. For twenty years, he had been married to Jane, the love of his life. Jane was a strong, caring woman who loved Dan very much. Jane managed the home, raised their son Kyle, actively volunteered her time in the community, and was very supportive of Dan's work and his career. Indeed, Dan had a very successful career; he was a successful writer, educator, and consultant. His book was selling very well, class after class was filled with students eager to understand his work and hear him speak, and consulting engagements were booked on his calendar several months in advance.

Dan's career required many long hours away from home with travel and the time required to keep his materials fresh and stimulating.

In addition to his passion for work, he was also passionate about his wife and son and had traditionally done whatever he could to stay engaged, striving for *quality* time at home since his work didn't always allow for *quantity*. Jane was content in her role as wife and mother and would help in the business office from time to time. Occasionally, Jane would push back and object to Dan's long hours or lack of attention to family matters. She had been able to step up and gently pull Dan's attention back to the family—until now, that is.

Jane's conflict started when Dan's business began to experience a growth spurt. Dan had set goals that would help him bring his work to more people through Internet forums by launching a new web site. He also began working day and night on a new management tool. Dan had a strong need to be involved at all levels of providing input and paying close attention to the many details throughout the development process. Dan's focus was on bringing the tool to market, and he seemed to have endless energy to devote to this work, leaving virtually no time or energy for home.

Jane had tried to be flexible and supportive during this time; however, it seemed all the responsibilities for the home and family were on her shoulders. Even on weekends when Jane expected to spend some quality time together, Dan was physically present, yet he was totally preoccupied with his work.

1

Now, six months after Dan's vision had been set into motion, the beta version of the management tool was nearly ready to be offered to a test market. This is when Jane invited me, her coach, to accompany her to Dan's office.

Dan was happy to see Jane and welcomed her with a warm kiss and hug. Dan opened the conversation and said, "This is perfect timing! I hope you are here to help celebrate the beta version of our new management tool. I'm really excited about this! Here, let me show you," he offered.

Jane was a little embarrassed by Dan's ingratiating enthusiasm and his lack of acknowledgment toward me. Jane interrupted, "Dan, I'd like you to meet someone."

"Oh, of course," Dan said apologetically. "I'm so sorry; I didn't mean to do that. It's just that this is a major turning point with this new product, and I'd love for you both to see it."

"Let me introduce my coach," Jane said firmly.

"Coach," Dan questioned. "I'm not sure I understand."

Jane replied, "Dan, please let me explain."

Looking puzzled, Dan paused to listen.

Jane started again. "This is Kathy, my coach. Several months ago, I mentioned to you that I was looking into hiring a coach. You supported the idea, and Kathy and I have been coaching once a week for the past three months."

After introductions, Jane continued, "Dan, your work has always been very important to you, and I accept that; it's important to me too. Somehow over the years, we have managed to spend enough time together as a family, and you have maintained a balance between work and home. However, since you've been working on launching the new web site and developing the new management tool, you haven't had time for your family. Kyle and I don't see you enough. I have felt neglected, and you missed Kyle's home game last night. Dan, I'm also worried about you—you look exhausted!"

"Kyle had a home game last night?" Dan asked slowly.

"Yes, Dan," Jane responded.

Dan always made it a priority to attend his son's home games whenever he was in town, and it was clear he felt dismayed having missed this opportunity to enjoy Kyle and watch his game.

"Dan," Jane continued, "even Stan, our next door neighbor, told me he has noticed a change."

"Why, I haven't talked with Stan in months?" Dan questioned.

"Yes, I know, Dan." Jane said sadly. "And the last time you did spend time with Stan he said all you talked about was what you were doing here at the office."

All of a sudden, Dan was sober and focused. Jane's words were soaking in. It was plain to see that Dan was truly troubled that Jane was unhappy.

"Dan, I have tried to get your attention and talk with you about all this, but you have been too absorbed in work and I didn't know how to approach you with my concerns. With the help of my coach, I'd like to talk with you now. Kathy has shown me how to use a Polarity Map, and I'd like to show you how it works. The Polarity Map has helped me see why work life needs to be balanced with home life, and I think it can help you understand this too," Jane said gently.

Jane and Dan both looked toward me. I looked at Dan.

"Dan, what are you feeling right now?" I asked.

"This was not a conversation I was expecting to have," he said sitting back in his chair. "My first reaction is to defend my focus on work, and yet I know Jane is right—I have been over focused on work, and neglecting home—neglecting Jane and Kyle", Dan paused and then slowly added, "I also feel over extended and it's having a negative impact on my work."

"Okay." Dan added looking at Jane. "I'm willing to listen."

Jane could see that Dan was open to feedback. Jane looked at me for encouragement as she laid the work and home map on the desk.

Dan looked at the map and cautiously asked, "Where do I start?"

Jane and I had worked through the Work and Home polarity together, and she was learning the key components of the Polarity Map. "Let's start here," Jane said pointing to the two ovals in the **Name the Poles** middle of the map. "I've written 'Work' in one oval, and 'Home' in the other. Kathy, can you explain?"

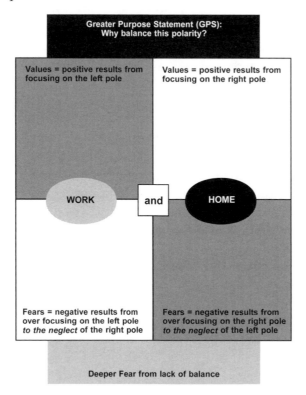

Polarity Map #1

"Sure," I said stepping in. "Work and Home are the interdependent poles of a polarity, and focusing solely on Home to the neglect of Work can cause a problem."

Dan nodded to affirm.

"And focusing solely on Work to the neglect of Home can also cause a problem," Jane added.

Dan took a deep breath and said, "Which is where we are at now. We are having a problem because I have over focused on Work."

Jane reached for Dan's hand.

I continued, "The objective of Polarity Management and Polarity Coaching is to identify what's needed to bring out the best of Work and the best of Home. A Polarity Map can help create a picture of where the tension is and identify what is needed to successfully manage the tension between work and home and provide a balance between the two."

Jane and I were silent for what felt like an awkward moment. Our eyes were on Dan. "Okay," Dan said, having thought it through. "Let's do this. Can we draw this on the white board?"

Jane smiled in relief, as I went to the white board and drew an outline of a Polarity Map with Work and Home in the ovals as the polarity to manage.

"Okay, let's look at the Polarity Map," I said. "There are four quadrants, divided by the left side, in this case the Work pole, and the right side, or Home pole of the Polarity Map. Let's begin with the Work pole. The word *work* holds personal value to each of us. What values are present for you when you think about work, Dan?" I asked.

Dan thought a moment and then answered, "First I'd say earning a living and providing for my family."

I wrote "Earn a living" in the upper left quadrant of work.

Upper Left Quadrant for Work

"I also find stimulation and growth through work challenges and being creative," Dan added.

As I wrote, Dan continued, "And, I also feel my work is a contribution to the business world and to academia, and that is important to me."

I glanced at Jane who smiled in agreement.

I finished writing and stepped away from the white board so that Dan and Jane could see the map.

"Are these your work values, Dan?" I asked.

"Yes, that sums it up quite well in those three bullets," Dan answered.

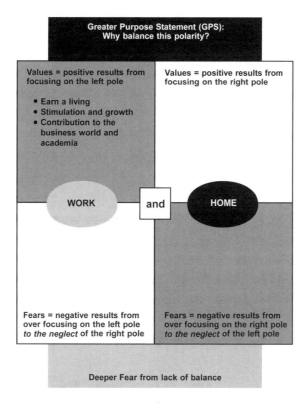

Polarity Map #2

"Work clearly brings some good things to your life, Dan. I am wondering if it is possible to get too much of a good thing?" I continued. "In other words, if you over focus on Work, to the neglect of Home, there is a downside. What comes to your mind here, Dan? What is the downside when you over focus on Work to the neglect of Home?"

Lower Left Quadrant for Work

After a moment of thought, Dan said, "I see that Jane has been unhappy with my focus on Work, and I missed Kyle's game last night—it wasn't even on my calendar, so I fear I have neglected my family."

Jane added, "and we haven't been out with friends or had anyone over for dinner since the management tool project began."

"You're right," Dan acknowledged.

I wrote neglected relationships with family and friends in the lower left quadrant.

"What else belongs in the downside of Work?" I asked.

Jane spoke up, "I'm worried about you, Dan, and I worry about your health. I don't think I've ever seen you looking so tired and worn out."

"I know you are right, Jane," Dan responded. "I am feeling burned out. I've been running on less than six hours of sleep for months, and I generally need more than that to be at the top of my game."

I continued to fill in the map. "Anything else?" I asked.

"Well, I have felt I've been all work and no play lately. Like Jane said, we haven't been out with friends, and I haven't played tennis in six months!" Dan added.

I wrote in "No time for personal interests."

"Is there anything else?" I asked.

Dan looked at Jane. "No, that's about it."

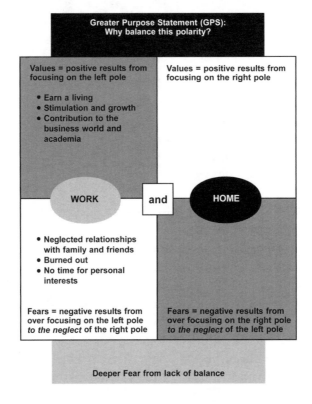

Polarity Map #3

As much as we needed to uncover the downside of Work, I could see Dan wasn't feeling good about what was on the white board. This was a good time to introduce the Infinity Loop and explain how in this process we were already following the Infinity Loop away from the downside of Work to the upside of Home.

"Before we go any further, I want to explain a basic principle of Polarity Management called the Infinity Loop." I drew an Infinity Loop on the map.

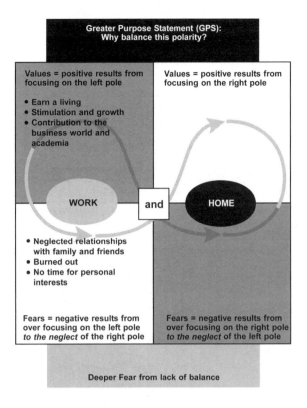

Polarity Map #4

"The Infinity Loop depicts the natural energy flow that holds the polarity together. Whether in balance or out of balance, it's always there and it takes us through one quadrant to the next. You see, when you reach the downside of Work, as we have here, the natural inclination is to begin moving to the upside of the other pole, which in this case is Home," I explained as I pointed to the loop and followed the pattern on the map with my hand.

Jane was also sensing Dan's negative reaction to the downside of work. Having been through this with me before, Jane interrupted politely. "Let's look at the upside of Home."

I looked at Dan. "Sure," he said, nodding in agreement.

"Okay. What is the upside of focus on Home? What are the values you hold there, Dan?" I asked.

Jane couldn't hold back. "Having quality time together with me and Kyle and time together with friends."

Upper Right Quadrant for Home

Dan looked at Jane with a big smile and said, "I agree."

It was good to see Dan smiling.

"Good," I said, as I began to fill in the upper right quadrant of the map.

"Yes, you're right, Jane," Dan continued. "And for me I would add that it would also be a break from work and a chance to refresh and renew myself. I could even get out to the tennis court."

I finished writing and stepped away from the white board.

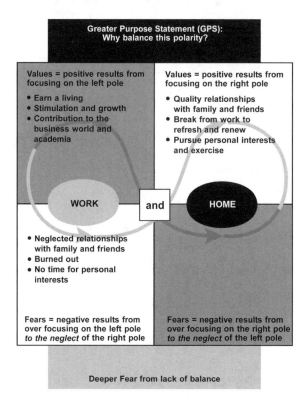

Polarity Map #5

"I'm not sure I'm going to like what comes next," Dan said, shaking his head, "no."

"Are you concerned about this being a reflection on me?" asked Jane.

"As much as I want to spend time with you, Jane, that's not all I need for a full life," Dan answered. "You know my life would be empty without you, Jane, and you know I also love my work."

"Of course, Dan," she acknowledged. "I know there is a downside to an over focus on home to the neglect of work. That's the beauty of what Polarity Management can show us. We can map

Lower Right Quadrant for Home

out the entire picture and achieve balance. Besides, if you didn't work we'd be broke," Jane teased.

"You may be right," Dan responded lightly. "There is a downside to over focus on Home to the neglect of Work. I hadn't thought of it like that."

I wrote the word *broke* on the Polarity Map.

"What else belongs on the downside of Home?" I asked.

Dan looked thoughtfully at the map. "If I follow the map and look at what we've written in the Work pole," Dan said slowly, "I can anticipate that I wouldn't have any challenges or opportunity to be creative and there would be a lack of stimulation and growth. Plus I would not be fulfilling my work vision of making the contributions to business and academia, and making those contributions is important to me."

I wrote as Dan spoke. "Does this look right?" I asked, stepping aside so that Jane and Dan could see the map clearly.

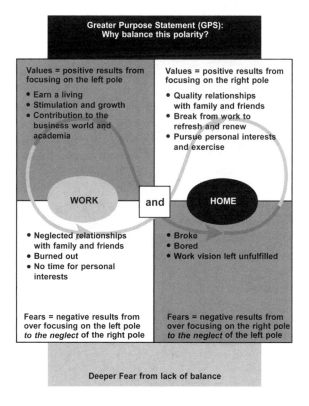

Polarity Map #6

"Yes, it does," Dan confirmed. "It makes sense to me that there has to be balance, and I can see now that I've been fighting against the balance for too long. But I still have a question."

"Of course," I encouraged.

"I might as well bring this up now. You see, I didn't know I was in the downside of Work, and I have to admit that sometimes I get so involved in what

I'm doing that I can see how I could get stuck in the down side of Work again. Although I don't really know I'm in the downside of Work, it does get harder and harder to stay upbeat and positive."

Jane gave a knowing nod.

"That's a great point, Dan," I said stepping back up to the white board. I drew in the "Vicious Cycle." "There's a part of the map that depicts what you were experiencing—it's called the Vicious Cycle. The Vicious Cycle spirals downward to the Deeper Fear at the bottom of the map because without balance, the Deeper Fear becomes more real. There is also a Virtuous Cycle that moves toward the Greater Purpose Statement at the top of the map," I said as I draw in the Virtuous Cycle. "When the polarity is in balance, there is upward movement."

Vicious and Virtuous Cycles

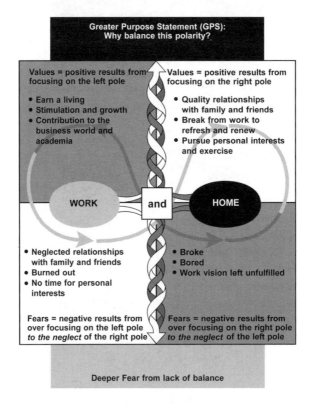

Polarity Map #7

"I can understand that," Dan said, "so how do I find the balance I need?"

"You find balance with Action Steps and Early Warnings," I answered and quickly added Action Steps and Early Warning sections to both sides of the map.

Maintaining a Full Life

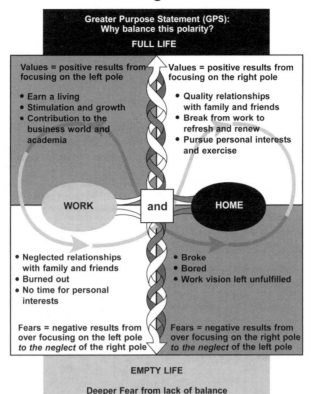

Action Steps

How will we gain or maintain the positive results from focusing on this left pole? What? Who? By when? Measures?

Action Steps

How will we gain or maintain the positive results from focusing on this right pole? What? Who? By when? Measures?

Greater Purpose Statement (GPS): Why balance this polarity?
FULL LIFE

Values = positive results from focusing on the left pole

- Earn a living
- Stimulation and growth
- Contribution to the business world and academia

Values = positive results from focusing on the right pole

- Quality relationships with family and friends
- Break from work to refresh and renew
- Pursue personal interests and exercise

WORK and **HOME**

Early Warnings

Measurable indicators (things you can count) that will let you know that you are getting into the downside of this left pole.

Early Warnings

Measurable indicators (things you can count) that will let you know that you are getting into the downside of this right pole.

- Neglected relationships with family and friends
- Burned out
- No time for personal interests

- Broke
- Bored
- Work vision left unfulfilled

Fears = negative results from over focusing on the left pole *to the neglect* of the right pole

Fears = negative results from over focusing on the right pole *to the neglect* of the left pole

EMPTY LIFE

Deeper Fear from lack of balance

Polarity Map #8

I continued, "Dan, you said that sometimes you get so involved in your work that you aren't aware that you are over focused on Work."

"That's right," Dan answered.

"And this has happened more than once?" I questioned.

"That's right," Dan said again.

"How do you know? What are the indicators or events that tell you that you have been over focused on Work and need to shift your focus to Home?" I asked.

> **Early Warnings due to an over focus on Work**

Dan smiled at Jane and said, "Jane tells me in one way or another. Or my staff will nudge me to go home and get some sleep, but usually Jane will tell me I look exhausted and that she's worried about me."

Jane returned the smile.

"Good, so you get feedback from Jane and your staff," I said as I wrote Dan's comments on the white board.

"Yes," Dan added. "And I hate to admit this, but when I'm really tired, sometimes I'm unable to concentrate on work; I forget things and miss commitments, like Kyle's game last night."

I finished adding these early warnings.

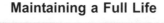

Maintaining a Full Life

Action Steps

How will we gain or maintain the positive results from focusing on this left pole? What? Who? By when? Measures?

Greater Purpose Statement (GPS):
Why balance this polarity?
FULL LIFE

Values = positive results from focusing on the left pole

- Earn a living
- Stimulation and growth
- Contribution to the business world and academia

Values = positive results from focusing on the right pole

- Quality relationships with family and friends
- Break from work to refresh and renew
- Pursue personal interests and exercise

Action Steps

How will we gain or maintain the positive results from focusing on this right pole? What? Who? By when? Measures?

WORK   and   HOME

Early Warnings

Measurable indicators (things you can count) that will let you know that you are getting into the downside of this left pole.

1. Jane tells me I look exhausted!
2. Staff tell me I need sleep.
3. I feel tired and unable to concentrate.
4. I forget things and miss commitments.

- Neglected relationships with family and friends
- Burned out
- No time for personal interests

Fears = negative results from over focusing on the left pole *to the neglect of the right pole*

- Broke
- Bored
- Work vision left unfulfilled

Fears = negative results from over focusing on the right pole *to the neglect of the left pole*

Early Warnings

Measurable indicators (things you can count) that will let you know that you are getting into the downside of this right pole.

EMPTY LIFE

Deeper Fear from lack of balance

Polarity Map #9

"So others recognize when you're on the downside of over focus on Work, and there are signals you pick up on?" I questioned to confirm.

Dan nodded to affirm.

"Okay, so what Action Steps can you take in response to the Early Warnings that we just talked about? What will you need to do to respond to those Early Warnings that occur from an over focus on Work?" I asked.

> **Action Steps**
> **to refocus on Home**

Dan looked at the map and thought for a few moments. Suddenly, he stood up and darted to the white board.

Taking the lead, he pointed to the Infinity Loop and smiled at Jane. Dan said, "I need to follow the Infinity Loop home, and I need to spend time with Jane. Jane, how about a date night?" Dan asked.

Returning the smile, Jane said, "How about a date night every week?"

Dan wrote it on the white board.

"Great!" I added, "It's good to get specific here."

Dan continued, "I would also like to play tennis once a week, and I would like to schedule some unplanned time each week when I could read, go for a walk, or be available to spend time with Kyle."

"I want to add something here!" Jane announced. "Focus on home should include a little time on the honey-do list."

"Okay, okay," Dan said as he somewhat reluctantly added Jane's request to the white board.

Dan stepped aside for Jane and me to see the map.

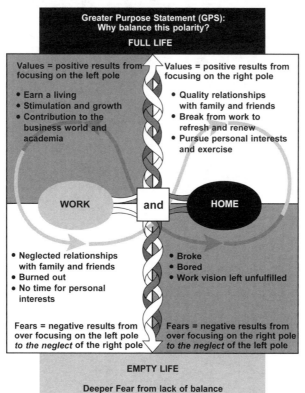

Polarity Map #10

"The next question is, what are the Early Warning signs that will signal me that I need to refocus on work," Dan pointed out.

"Right," I acknowledged.

"I think an Early Warning would be that money is tight," Jane said jumping in.

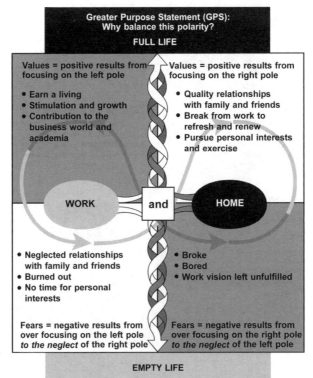

Early Warnings due to an over focus on Home

Dan nodded his head with certainty and began recording on the white board.

"That means I have to get busy!" Dan added. "Money gets tight when there's no work on my calendar," Dan added.

"I also know that I would miss the stimulation and the challenge of work if I over focus on Home, and I would have guilt feelings about not making contributions to businesses and to my students."

"You know yourself pretty well, Dan," I recognized.

"Yes, I've lived with myself a long time," Dan joked as he finished that section of the map.

Maintaining a Full Life

Action Steps

How will we gain or maintain the positive results from focusing on this left pole? What? Who? By when? Measures?

Greater Purpose Statement (GPS):
Why balance this polarity?
FULL LIFE

Values = positive results from focusing on the left pole

Values = positive results from focusing on the right pole

- Earn a living
- Stimulation and growth
- Contribution to the business world and academia

- Quality relationships with family and friends
- Break from work to refresh and renew
- Pursue personal interests and exercise

WORK and **HOME**

Action Steps

How will we gain or maintain the positive results from focusing on this right pole? What? Who? By when? Measures?

1. Date night once a week.
2. Play tennis once a week.
3. Schedule unplanned time.
4. "Honey-do" list.

Early Warnings

Measurable indicators (things you can count) that will let you know that you are getting into the downside of this left pole.

- Neglected relationships with family and friends
- Burned out
- No time for personal interests

- Broke
- Bored
- Work vision left unfulfilled

Early Warnings

Measurable indicators (things you can count) that will let you know that you are getting into the downside of this right pole.

1. Jane tells me I look exhausted!
2. Staff tell me I need sleep.
3. I feel tired and unable to concentrate.
4. I forget things and miss commitments.

Fears = negative results from over focusing on the left pole *to the neglect* of the right pole

Fears = negative results from over focusing on the right pole *to the neglect* of the left pole

1. Money is tight.
2. Not much work on the calendar.
3. Miss stimulation and challenge of work.
4. Feeling guilty and not contributing.

EMPTY LIFE

Deeper Fear from lack of balance

Polarity Map #11

Dan pushed forward, "So what will be the Action Steps I need to take to move back to the upside of Work?"

Action Steps to refocus on Work

Dan thought for a few moments and then answered his own question, "There are several things. I need to follow up with potential clients so that I have work on my calendar; that's an easy one. I also have a tendency to over commit; for example, I want to make sure I'm teaching no more than one course each semester. I can easily be persuaded to teach more than one, and every time I do, I feel I've overcommitted and experience overload. I also need to follow the work plans I've created for my new web site and the management tool; that should be easy, and doing that will help me be clearer about any changes to the plan that I decide to make."

Dan looked at the list, "I'll add another." Dan said after a brief pause, "Although it's a little outside my comfort zone, I need to delegate more so that I can target the things that are most important for me from a work perspective, and will free up time that could be invested in either Work or Home. I see this one as a win-win!"

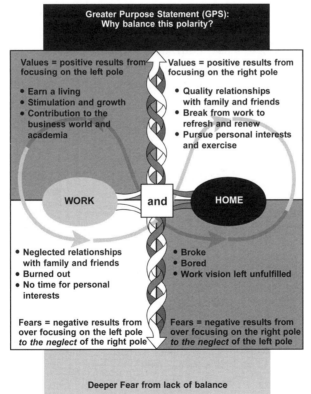

Action Steps

How will we gain or maintain the positive results from focusing on this left pole? What? Who? By when? Measures?

1. Follow up with potential clients on regular basis.
2. Avoid tendency to over-commit.
3. Stick to work plans and be clear about changes.
4. Delegate more!

Early Warnings

Measurable indicators (things you can count) that will let you know that you are getting into the downside of this left pole.

1. Jane tells me I look exhausted!
2. Staff tell me I need sleep.
3. I feel tired and unable to concentrate.
4. I forget things and miss commitments.

Greater Purpose Statement (GPS): Why balance this polarity?

Values = positive results from focusing on the left pole

- Earn a living
- Stimulation and growth
- Contribution to the business world and academia

Values = positive results from focusing on the right pole

- Quality relationships with family and friends
- Break from work to refresh and renew
- Pursue personal interests and exercise

WORK and **HOME**

- Neglected relationships with family and friends
- Burned out
- No time for personal interests

- Broke
- Bored
- Work vision left unfulfilled

Fears = negative results from over focusing on the left pole *to the neglect* of the right pole

Fears = negative results from over focusing on the right pole *to the neglect* of the left pole

Deeper Fear from lack of balance

Action Steps

How will we gain or maintain the positive results from focusing on this right pole? What? Who? By when? Measures?

1. Date night once a week.
2. Play tennis once a week.
3. Schedule unplanned time.
4. "Honey-do" list.

Early Warnings

Measurable indicators (things you can count) that will let you know that you are getting into the downside of this right pole.

1. Money is tight.
2. Not much work on the calendar.
3. Miss stimulation and challenge of work.
4. Feeling guilty and not contributing.

Polarity Map #12

Dan moved back to the chair next to Jane's and sat down. We all admired the map together.

"There's one more thing," I added. "We talked earlier about the Greater Purpose and the Deeper Fear."

"Yes," said Dan, "I was wondering about that."

"Let's look at that now," I said. "Dan, I've heard you say that you have a full life. Is that true?"

"Yes," Dan answered. "I have a wonderfully full life, with Jane, my work, our home, our son, and our friends. I wouldn't have it any other way."

"Jane, what do you think?" I asked.

"I agree. I didn't marry Dan because he liked to sit around," Jane supported.

"In the Greater Purpose box on the top of the map is a place to write what you are striving for," I said. "And the box below the map is what you want to avoid, the Deeper Fear. What are you striving for, Dan?" I asked. "What do you see as your Greater Purpose?"

Greater Purpose

"I want to experience a full life—a full work life and a full home life." Dan answered, "Yes, I want to have a full life."

I wrote "Full Life" in the box on top of the map. "And what do you want to avoid; what is your Deeper Fear, Dan?" I asked.

"Like I said earlier, without Jane, my son, my home, and my work, my life would be empty."

"Okay, sounds like an empty life may be the Deeper Fear. Do you agree with that?" I asked.

Deeper Fear

"Yes, that makes sense to me," Dan responded.

"I like it," added Jane.

I wrote "Empty Life" in the box on the bottom of the map.

And finally on the top of the map I wrote "Maintaining a Full Life." This is what it's all about," I said as I wrote.

Name the Map

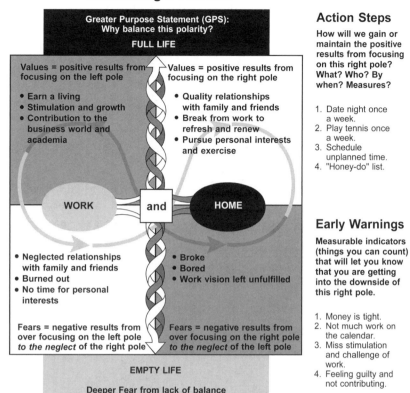

Maintaining a Full Life

Action Steps

How will we gain or maintain the positive results from focusing on this left pole? What? Who? By when? Measures?

1. Follow up with potential clients on regular basis.
2. Avoid tendency to over-commit.
3. Stick to work plans and be clear about changes.
4. Delegate more!

Early Warnings

Measurable indicators (things you can count) that will let you know that you are getting into the downside of this left pole.

1. Jane tells me I look exhausted!
2. Staff tell me I need sleep.
3. I feel tired and unable to concentrate.
4. I forget things and miss commitments.

Greater Purpose Statement (GPS): Why balance this polarity?
FULL LIFE

Values = positive results from focusing on the left pole

- Earn a living
- Stimulation and growth
- Contribution to the business world and academia

Values = positive results from focusing on the right pole

- Quality relationships with family and friends
- Break from work to refresh and renew
- Pursue personal interests and exercise

WORK **and** HOME

- Neglected relationships with family and friends
- Burned out
- No time for personal interests

- Broke
- Bored
- Work vision left unfulfilled

Fears = negative results from over focusing on the left pole *to the neglect* of the right pole

Fears = negative results from over focusing on the right pole *to the neglect* of the left pole

EMPTY LIFE
Deeper Fear from lack of balance

Action Steps

How will we gain or maintain the positive results from focusing on this right pole? What? Who? By when? Measures?

1. Date night once a week.
2. Play tennis once a week.
3. Schedule unplanned time.
4. "Honey-do" list.

Early Warnings

Measurable indicators (things you can count) that will let you know that you are getting into the downside of this right pole.

1. Money is tight.
2. Not much work on the calendar.
3. Miss stimulation and challenge of work.
4. Feeling guilty and not contributing.

Polarity Map #13

Jane said proudly, "This is how we will find balance, Dan. This is how we can manage our work-home polarity."

Dan nodded to confirm. "I think I'll have this framed, but right now I think you and I should take our first Action Step toward balancing the upside of home. Where would you like to go to dinner tonight, Jane?"

I said good-bye to Jane and Dan that afternoon, and the next week at our regularly scheduled time, Jane spoke with more hope and energy than she had in weeks.

"I really feel the wall between Dan and me has come down, Kathy. We are open with each other again and able to communicate," Jane said. "We are both grateful for the Polarity Coaching and for the Polarity Map."

~

This first case has introduced you to a common polarity, Home and Work, and how Polarity Coaching provides a systematic walk through the Polarity Map. As a coach, you can use this process to work with clients who have difficulty managing the Home and Work polarity and help them uncover their own values, fears, actions steps, and early warnings.

~

The next case is based on a challenging polarity faced by many, caring for self and caring for others. This polarity is often difficult to see and difficult to manage, and too often a person can live in the downside of caring for others to the point of complete exhaustion. As Lisa's story unfolds, the positive and negative aspects of the polarity she is living comes into focus, and it is at that point she can be intentional about her time and her focus on self and others.

Case Study #2
Care of Self and Others

Lisa and Jack's marriage started as so many marriages do, with a lovely bride and a handsome groom ready to start their lives together. They had a deep love, a solid relationship, and a bright future.

Jack had been working in the family business, and after the wedding, Lisa began a new job working in the headquarters office of a major bank. Five years passed, and they felt ready to start a family. They had discussed this often and had agreed that when the day came for a child, Lisa would quit her job to be a stay-at-home mom. She loved the idea of managing their home and taking care of her husband and children. When Lisa and Jack found out they were pregnant, they were elated! Lisa quit her job when their daughter was born, and she began to fulfill her dream of caring for others as a wife and mother.

Lisa focused all her energy on taking care of the baby and her husband and managing their home. Jack had always been a hard worker and now, as the only breadwinner and with a new baby, he was even more dedicated to long hours on the job. The seasons turned, and Lisa was happy in her role; she was proud of her ability to care for their daughter, and she loved her husband and felt life was good.

Lisa and Jack knew they wanted more than one child, and three and a half years later, their second daughter was born. Now with two children to care for, things became more difficult. The needs of a 3½-year-old had to be met, while caring for an infant. With two children in the home, Lisa could not sleep when the baby slept, and her energy began to deplete. She was tired most of the time and had little time to focus on herself. Jack got less attention at home, and this caused some stress; the budget was tight, and he spent more time than ever at work. Even with the stress of a second child and managing the home with little time from Jack, Lisa continued to keep things going; she continued to care for others.

Despite a very busy life, Lisa and Jack felt their family was not yet complete. Two years later, their third baby, another girl, was born. A more picture perfect family could not be found, and Lisa knew how blessed she was.

About this same time, Jack left his position in the family-owned business, and with the drive and energy of a young entrepreneur, he started a business of his own. This put even more responsibility for the family on Lisa, and over time, her ability to care for others the way she had envisioned became more and more difficult to maintain. She was always tired. She became overwhelmed and complained about the fact that Jack was rarely home. She often felt as though for every one step forward that she made, the needs of others pulled her two steps back. She finally got to a point where she knew something had to change, she just didn't know what. That's when Lisa called a coach.

We met for the first time, and after discussing the formalities of our coaching relationship, I asked permission to take notes, and we got started.

Lisa seemed cautious. She let me know right away that one of her core values was staying home to raise her children and that she was proud of being a stay-at-home mom. She made it clear that if I was going to suggest that she put the girls in day care, or get a job outside the home, that was not going to happen.

"Lisa, as your coach, I will ask questions, listen, encourage, support, and challenge you. I will hold you accountable to take the action steps you choose to reach your life goals. Your role will be to explore your goals and desires at a deep level, be resourceful, take action, and learn through this process as together we see and celebrate the changes you make in your life," I said sincerely.

This seemed to put Lisa at ease. "Okay, that sounds good," she said as she relaxed back in her chair.

"Here's the problem," Lisa began, "I am finding more and more that I cannot do it all. It feels as if I don't have a minute for myself and I feel resentful that my entire day is spent on doing things for my family. Don't misunderstand, I love my family and they are the most important thing in my life, but day after day, I never seem to get a break!"

As Lisa told her story, I could hear her strong value of caring for her family and I could hear her need to care for herself. I began sketching a Polarity Map as what Lisa was describing was a classic polarity to manage—caring for others and caring for self.

Name the Poles

I opened by honoring what I felt Lisa had been honoring since their first baby was born, caring for others.

"Lisa, tell me about your life. What are you most proud of?" I asked.

Lisa started with her girls. "They are all three bright and beautiful, yet unique in their own way. I love watching them learn and grow not only in school, but also in dance and music. I enjoy the simple things with them, like being able to fix their hair, answering their questions, shopping for cute clothes, and watching them play in the yard. My family comes first," she emphasized, "and my goal is to have a family-centered home—a place where all their friends love to come and hang out, especially as the girls get older. I really want to enjoy these years, as I know they will pass quickly."

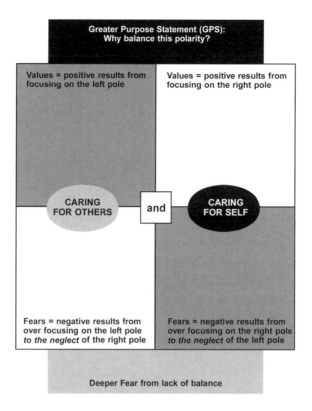

Polarity Map #1

Lisa paused and then continued, "I'm also very proud of Jack; he has worked really hard to establish a solid customer base for his business and his hard work is beginning to pay off, but he's not at a point where he can hire the help he needs to take some of the pressure off, so he needs my help from time-to-time, and I've tried to be there for him."

As Lisa talked about what she was most proud of, I began filling in the Polarity Map. I listened for the values that Lisa held dear while caring for others and started to make notes. Her

> **Upper Left Quadrant for Caring for Others**

family came first, and their health and well-being, the girls' education, and now that they were older, their extra curricular activities were also important to her. Her desire was to enjoy these years while the girls were growing up, and she also wanted to be a supportive partner for her husband as he built his business.

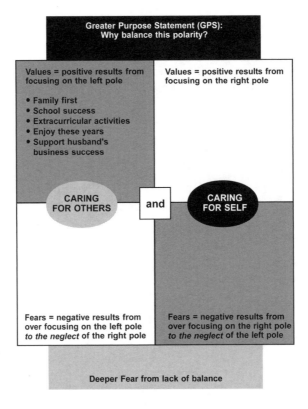

**Greater Purpose Statement (GPS):
Why balance this polarity?**

Values = positive results from focusing on the left pole

- Family first
- School success
- Extracurricular activities
- Enjoy these years
- Support husband's business success

Values = positive results from focusing on the right pole

CARING FOR OTHERS   and   CARING FOR SELF

Fears = negative results from over focusing on the left pole *to the neglect* of the right pole

Fears = negative results from over focusing on the right pole *to the neglect* of the left pole

Deeper Fear from lack of balance

Polarity Map #2

When Lisa stopped speaking, we sat for a moment as her heart-felt words soaked in.

Then I continued, "That is a beautiful picture, Lisa, and I can see how grounded you are in these values. I have to ask, however, what toll is this taking?"

I could sense from Lisa's expression that this was a hard question to answer. After a brief pause she went on.

"I'm spent—just worn down. I give everything I have and it's never enough," she said sadly. "It takes all my time and energy to stay focused and keep everything moving in the right

> **Lower Left Quadrant
> for Caring for Others**

direction. I don't get enough help from the girls or from Jack, and I have a hard time maintaining the home and keeping the schedule. Sometimes I feel my whole life revolves around the girls and Jack, and that I've lost myself. I just don't feel I have a life of my own anymore, or a life with my husband, and when this happens I start shutting down."

Lisa looked down at her hands; her words were full of emotion as she reflected on the difficulties of caring for others. "I feel guilty for letting this happen," she said as she blinked back the tears. "I realize how blessed I am, and I love my family. I don't want to be in this place, but it's just very hard right now," Lisa said softly.

We both sat quietly for a few moments to acknowledge the emotion. When Lisa was ready to continue, I filled in the downside of caring for others on the Polarity Map with what I had heard.

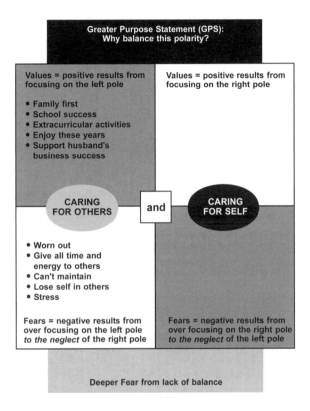

Polarity Map #3

"Are you ready to go on, Lisa?" I asked.

"Yes, I'm ready. I guess I've got some emotion bottled up inside around all this," Lisa acknowledged. "I'm fine, really, let's continue," Lisa urged.

"Okay. Let's focus on you, Lisa," I said. "Now think big and bold—what would you like to have that you don't have now?"

"Oh, I guess that could be a lot of things, like a maid—that would be good!" As Lisa spoke her body straightened and a smile came to her face. "I'd like to get my hair done, or better yet, my hair and my nails, a complete makeover. Or, how about a month on a deserted island with only magazines and chocolate as companions," she said lightly.

"That's good." I said, enjoying Lisa's fun with the brainstorming exercise.

"What would this look like? How would you feel?" I asked.

Lisa thought carefully. "Realistically, I think first I need to take better care of myself physically," she replied. "I'd like to get more physically fit, and I think I'd have more energy overall if I could do that."

"Good. What else?" I asked as I wrote the words "Fitness focus" in the upper right quadrant of the Polarity Map.

Upper Right Quadrant for Caring for Self

"This is easier said than done, but I need to have a system, some sort of schedule, that allows me to get away from being needed 24/7, day after day," she said. "I know the girls are old enough now to help with some things, and I need more help from Jack. I need to establish chores for the girls and work on establishing some new habits with them. And I've got to talk to Jack about picking up after himself."

Lisa seemed to gain energy as she spoke, "I need to develop interests of my own and with Jack as a couple. I don't really have interests outside the home and I need to take a class or find a hobby. Maybe Jack and I could find something we are both interested in—we've lost that time together, and I'm not happy about that. I would love to have a date night with Jack again. Yes, and I remember when I felt happier and life was more satisfying—I want that again," Lisa said with emphasis.

"It sounds like you have a clear picture of what you want!" I said as I continued writing in the values quadrant of caring for self.

Before going on, I felt this was a good time to share the Polarity Map I had been sketching with Lisa.

"Lisa, I'd like to stop here a moment and show you what I've been sketching in my notes. I've started creating a map of what we've talked about today," I said.

I laid it out in front of her.

"This is called a Polarity Map," I said, as I started to explain. "Polarity Management is a tool I use with my coaching clients when tension exists and there are issues that seem to be unsolvable. Once the map is filled out, we can look at both the positive results and negative effects of the tension," I explained as Lisa looked at the map curiously.

"The map has two poles, the two ovals, and based on our discussion, I think the poles that are causing the tension are Caring for Others and Caring for Self," I continued.

"Let's look at it this way." I offered as I covered the right side of the map, Caring for Self, with a piece of paper and drew her attention to the top left quadrant of the map, the values section of caring for others.

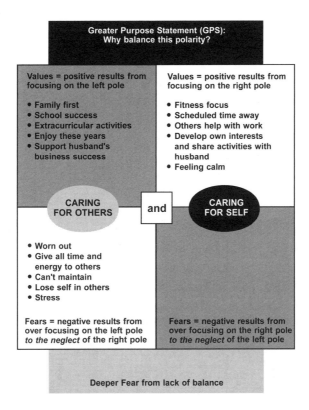

Polarity Map #4

"I'd like to confirm what I heard you say, Lisa," I said.

"Sure, this looks interesting," Lisa answered.

"I heard that Caring for Others in your family is your focus and that your family is first and most important in your life."

Lisa nodded in agreement.

"I also heard that school success for the girls and providing the right environment for your family to enjoy and prosper are important. I heard that giving your husband support in his business venture is also important."

Lisa read the list and agreed that these were the values she held to every day. "Yes, living out these family values is paramount to me," she replied.

I made a note—Greater Purpose may be living out family values.

I explained to Lisa that I felt her over focus on the Caring for Others had caused her to move to the lower left quadrant of the Polarity Map.

As I read through the list in the lower left quadrant of the map, Lisa acknowledged that these were the negative impacts she was experiencing and that her deeper fear came from the fact that she often felt herself living in this negative place and losing hold of her values.

I made another side note: Deeper Fear = not living out family values.

Then I uncovered the right side of the Polarity Map and, pointing to the Caring for Self pole, I refocused our attention to the top quadrant of the Caring for Self pole.

We talked again about Lisa's desire to become more physically fit and that doing this would bring her more energy. It would also take time away from the family, and she acknowledged this could be good for her and good for the family. We talked about others taking responsibility to pick up after themselves and being assigned chores; Lisa had some ideas and she made some notes about how that might work. Lisa spoke about her own interests and how she had enjoyed ceramics before the girls were born. She also pointed out that the dirt bikes Jack bought when they were newlyweds had been in the garage unused for many years; "This could be the common activity I'm looking for," she thought out loud as she wrote her ideas on paper.

Lisa looked at the list again, "If these things were in place, I would have some time for myself and I think I would be happier. I would feel like I had a piece of myself back again."

"Good," I answered. "Now there's another quadrant to fill in, which is over focus on Caring for Self to the neglect of Caring for Others."

This seemed foreign to Lisa. She seemed to shift back in her chair as if to move away from the prospect of over focusing on her self. I realized that before going on this would be a good time to introduce the Infinity Loop.

Infinity Loop

"Before we look at the lower right quadrant, let me introduce you to the Infinity Loop," I said as I drew in the Infinity Loop on the Polarity Map.

"The Infinity Loop is the force that moves us through the quadrants of the Polarity Map," I continued. "It's a natural movement that requires us to focus on Caring for Others and Caring for Self over time."

Lisa looked confused.

"Let me give you an example." I went on, "You have been focused on Caring for Others and living out these values." I pointed to the upper left-hand quadrant. "And, I hear you say you feel yourself experiencing the downside of this focus, which is being worn down, giving all your time and energy to others, causing you to shut down, etc." With my finger on the map, I followed the Infinity Loop to the lower quadrant of Caring for Others. "This is naturally what you will experience when you over focus on Caring for Others to the neglect of Caring for Self. This is the energy force that moves from the upside or the values part of Caring for Others, to the downside or the fears part of Caring for Others.

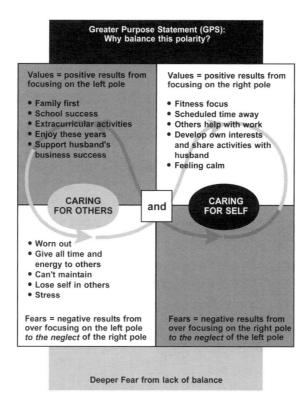

Polarity Map #5

"Yes, I am fighting that all the time, struggling to stay on the upside," Lisa confessed.

I continued to follow the loop to the upside of Caring for Self. "And when we talked about Caring for Self, you began to brainstorm and you seemed energized talking about what you could do for yourself, how you could do it, and how it would feel. Is that right?" I asked.

"Yes, that's right, I did," Lisa agreed. "I would love to focus on myself for a change and get away, and then Jack and the girls would have to pick up after themselves and take care of the house," she replied almost defensively.

"That's what I want, but not all I want," she added pointing to the values written in the upside of caring for others.

"Exactly!" I responded. "We can see the upside of Caring for Self, but when you follow the Infinity Loop, what happens?" I asked. "What would happen if you were to over focus on Caring for Self to the neglect of Caring for Others?"

The downside of Caring for Self to the neglect of caring for Others was clearer to Lisa now.

"That is hard to think about," Lisa said after thinking for a moment.

"Worst case scenario?" Lisa asked.

"Okay, worst case," I answered.

"Well, this doesn't sound good, but if I focus on myself to the neglect of others, my needs would come first. I wouldn't have time to help the girls with their homework, and there wouldn't be anyone to take the girls to dance class and music lessons. I really wouldn't be happier because my family is my real joy. And, worse case scenario, Jack would be picking up my responsibilities and his business would be neglected," Lisa said strongly. "And, that is not what I really want either. I know that if that happened because I was over focused on myself, I wouldn't really be living any of my values."

> **Lower Right Quadrant for Caring for Self**

Lisa finished speaking and I finished the lower right quadrant of the Polarity Map. Then I explained that what I heard her say about family values being paramount to her and living out those family values is the vision, or the Greater Purpose, she is striving for and I wrote "Live Out Family Values" in the rectangle above the map, and that her Deeper Fear is not living out those family values, or losing site of family values. I wrote "Lose Site of Family Values" in the rectangle below the map.

> **Greater Purpose**

> **Deeper Fear**

"You see, Lisa, it's possible to maintain balance between the two poles if you can view both poles as an interdependent pair to be managed over time, then you can create a natural Virtuous Cycle toward the greater purpose of living out your family values. If you are unable to maintain balance and over focus on one to the neglect of the other, then a Vicious Cycle begins a downward spiral.

> **Virtuous and Vicious Cycles**

I drew in the Virtuous Cycle and the Vicious Cycle spirals.

I turned the Polarity Map around for Lisa to see.

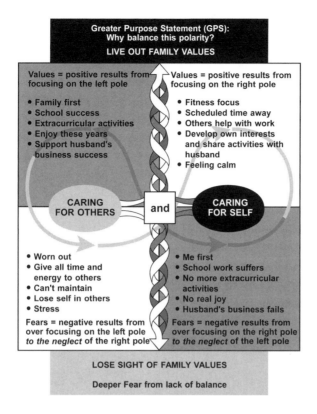

Greater Purpose Statement (GPS):
Why balance this polarity?
LIVE OUT FAMILY VALUES

Values = positive results from focusing on the left pole

- Family first
- School success
- Extracurricular activities
- Enjoy these years
- Support husband's business success

Values = positive results from focusing on the right pole

- Fitness focus
- Scheduled time away
- Others help with work
- Develop own interests and share activities with husband
- Feeling calm

CARING FOR OTHERS **and** **CARING FOR SELF**

- Worn out
- Give all time and energy to others
- Can't maintain
- Lose self in others
- Stress

Fears = negative results from over focusing on the left pole *to the neglect* of the right pole

- Me first
- School work suffers
- No more extracurricular activities
- No real joy
- Husband's business fails

Fears = negative results from over focusing on the right pole *to the neglect* of the left pole

LOSE SIGHT OF FAMILY VALUES

Deeper Fear from lack of balance

Polarity Map #6

Lisa looked confused again, so I explained, "As you experience the downside of caring for others and you recognize this is not a good place to be, you begin to see the upside of caring for yourself. Now Caring for Self is a good thing, but there is also a downside to over focusing on Caring for Self to the neglect of Caring for Others, which is what will happen if the polarity isn't managed well over time. Either way, you can get caught in a Vicious Cycle. What would happen if you spent too much time working out, took too much time away from home, expected more from your family than they could reasonably give, and spent the majority of your time on your own interests and demanded time from your husband that maybe wasn't reasonable?"

"You can forget the happier life," Lisa exclaimed. "I see what you mean. It would jeopardize everything I've worked for and what I value and what Jack is working for and what he values. My whole family would suffer. I can't only focus on my needs and what I want to the neglect of others. I don't want to lose sight of the family values that are important to me and to Jack. In fact, I'd miss some of the joy of the best years of my life, and that would be the opposite of what I really want!" Lisa insisted.

Lisa studied the Polarity Map, and then said, "So a Virtuous Cycle is at work when the polarity is managed and in balance over time."

"Yes," I answered quickly, "When you maintain balance, it happens naturally."

Finally she said, "This makes so much sense! I can see that if I over focus on Caring for Others, over time it really isn't a benefit to me or to my family." Lisa stressed. "And, if I were to over focus on myself, that wouldn't benefit me or my family either. I can see that I need to bring balance between Caring for Others and Caring for Self into my life. But, how can that happen?" Lisa asked. "If I follow the Infinity Loop, it will lead to the downside of the poles."

"There is a way to bring balance into your life," I reassured her as I drew in the outline for Action Steps and Early Warnings.

"This is where Action Steps and Early Warnings come in," I explained.

Action Steps

How will we gain or maintain the positive results from focusing on this left pole? What? Who? By when? Measures?

Greater Purpose Statement (GPS): Why balance this polarity? LIVE OUT FAMILY VALUES

Values = positive results from focusing on the left pole

- Family first
- School success
- Extracurricular activities
- Enjoy these years
- Support husband's business success

Values = positive results from focusing on the right pole

- Fitness focus
- Scheduled time away
- Others help with work
- Develop own interests and share activities with husband
- Feeling calm

CARING FOR OTHERS and **CARING FOR SELF**

Action Steps

How will we gain or maintain the positive results from focusing on this right pole? What? Who? By when? Measures?

Early Warnings

Measurable indicators (things you can count) that will let you know that you are getting into the downside of this left pole.

- Worn out
- Give all time and energy to others
- Can't maintain
- Lose self in others
- Stress

Fears = negative results from over focusing on the left pole *to the neglect* of the right pole

- Me first
- School work suffers
- No more extracurricular activities
- No real joy
- Husband's business fails

Fears = negative results from over focusing on the right pole *to the neglect* of the left pole

Early Warnings

Measurable indicators (things you can count) that will let you know that you are getting into the downside of this right pole.

LOSE SIGHT OF FAMILY VALUES

Deeper Fear from lack of balance

Polarity Map #7

We looked at the Polarity Map again. I explained that Early Warnings are indicators that allow you to anticipate and respond to downside experiences quickly, before the negative effects of that downside adversely change the situation; they signal the need to move back to the Action Steps of the interdependent pole. Action Steps are specific and can be measurable to provide a structure for accountability and self-correction. Responding to Early Warnings with the appropriate Action Steps keeps the Infinity Loop in the upside of the two poles.

"Does that make sense?" I asked.

"Yes, I think I understand," Lisa answered.

"Let's start where you are at right now. Where are you on the Infinity Loop?" I asked.

Lisa put her finger on the Infinity Loop and traced it from the upside of Caring for Others to just below the line inside the lower quadrant of Caring for Others.

"So you believe you are moving from the upside or values quadrant of Caring for Others to the downside or fear quadrant of Caring for Others?"

Lisa gave a slow, but affirming nod.

"How do you know this, Lisa?" I asked

"It seems like I'm tired all the time. With all I have to do, it really is difficult for me to get enough rest," Lisa responded.

Early Warnings due to an over focus on Caring for Others

"That's what we're looking for," I encouraged.

"So, an Early Warning would be lack of sleep?" Lisa asked.

"Yes, and now how can you make it measurable?" I asked. "How much rest do you need to feel good?"

"Well, I would like to get an average of seven hours of sleep per night and I haven't been able to do that for a long time. I'd also like to be able to take a restful break and sit in the sun for 30 minutes on a beautiful day like today."

"How often would you like to sun?" I asked.

"Oh, every day, but if that's not possible then maybe three or four times a week."

"Great. What else?" I asked as I wrote in "< 7 hours sleep each night and sun < 30 min., 3 days per week."

"I need Jack to help me with the girls at night. Making dinner, helping with homework, after school running to music lessons and dance: I really need some help there," she said.

"How much help?" I asked.

"Tuesday through Thursday are the important nights, and if he could be available even for two or three hours, that would really help!" Lisa stated.

I wrote in "Jack available < 2 hours school nights, Tuesday through Thursday."

"Anything else?" I asked.

"Yes," she said firmly. "I'm not sure how this fits, but I'm going to create a schedule of chores for the girls and include a point system so that each time they do one of the chores they are assigned, they earn points. Points could equate to allowance or privileges."

"Okay, we can look at the specifics of that later," I said and wrote "point system," with an asterisk notation for more specifics to come. "Anything else?" I asked.

"Not to start with," Lisa replied.

"Let's take another look," I said turning the map around for Lisa to view.

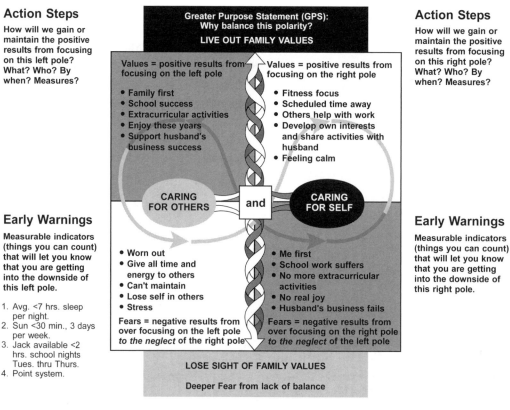

Polarity Map #8

"So these Early Warnings will help me see when I could be heading toward the downside of Caring for Others, right?" Lisa questioned.

"That's right." When you start experiencing these Early Warning signs, you need to take some action. Let's move along the Infinity Loop and focus on the upside of Caring for Self. In other words, what action steps will you take to balance Caring for Others with Caring for Self?" I asked.

> **Action Steps to refocus on Caring for Self**

"Oh, this is hard," Lisa paused. "I guess I'd need to get seven hours of sleep, and keeping with the fitness focus, I'd like to exercise three or four times a week. I could jog or ride bike for an hour to get that in. I guess if I'm coming from the downside of Caring for Others, that means Jack isn't helping out, and the point system has fallen by the wayside. I'd have to reenlist Jack and reinforce and manage the point system better."

"That's right! You are really seeing how this works," I affirmed.

Lisa continued, "I also want to have a night to myself at least once a month to take a class, or go to the moms' night out that's often scheduled for the moms in the neighborhood. And Jack and I need a date night at least twice a month."

I wrote in the Action Steps for caring for self and showed it to Lisa.

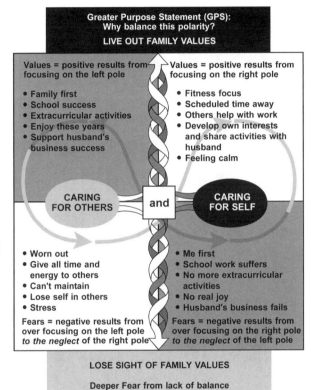

Action Steps

How will we gain or maintain the positive results from focusing on this left pole? What? Who? By when? Measures?

Greater Purpose Statement (GPS): Why balance this polarity?
LIVE OUT FAMILY VALUES

Values = positive results from focusing on the left pole

Values = positive results from focusing on the right pole

- Family first
- School success
- Extracurricular activities
- Enjoy these years
- Support husband's business success

- Fitness focus
- Scheduled time away
- Others help with work
- Develop own interests and share activities with husband
- Feeling calm

Action Steps

How will we gain or maintain the positive results from focusing on this right pole? What? Who? By when? Measures?

1. 7 hrs. sleep each night.
2. Exercise 4 times per week.
3. Re-enlist Jack's help.
4. Manage point system.
5. 1 night out per month.
6. 2 date nights per month.

CARING FOR OTHERS and **CARING FOR SELF**

Early Warnings

Measurable indicators (things you can count) that will let you know that you are getting into the downside of this left pole.

- Worn out
- Give all time and energy to others
- Can't maintain
- Lose self in others
- Stress

- Me first
- School work suffers
- No more extracurricular activities
- No real joy
- Husband's business fails

Fears = negative results from over focusing on the left pole *to the neglect of the right pole*

Fears = negative results from over focusing on the right pole *to the neglect of the left pole*

Early Warnings

Measurable indicators (things you can count) that will let you know that you are getting into the downside of this right pole.

1. Avg. <7 hrs. sleep per night.
2. Sun <30 min., 3 days per week.
3. Jack available <2 hrs. school nights Tues. thru Thurs.
4. Point system.

LOSE SIGHT OF FAMILY VALUES

Deeper Fear from lack of balance

Polarity Map #9

"Wow, look at this. I could really get into this life style!" Lisa said excitedly.

"And working these Action Steps on the map can help you get positive results from Caring for Self and work toward achieving balance," I added.

"Oh yes, balance," Lisa looked thoughtfully, "because if I over focused on myself, I'd move to the downside of Caring for Self," Lisa continued. "Okay, I get it. I need some Early Warnings so that I know if I'm over focusing on Caring for Self to the neglect of Caring for Others."

Early Warnings due to an over focus on Caring for Self

"Exactly!" I affirmed.

"Okay, well, the girls wouldn't have me to oversee their homework, so I suspect some of the homework would go unfinished," she said. "It could interfere with getting them to their music and dance lessons. I'd feel really bad about that, and so would they. And, if I pulled Jack away from work too often, he could start missing deadlines and that could have serious consequences for his business. Plus sometimes he needs my help, and if I'm not able to help it can be really difficult for him."

I wrote in the Early Warnings.

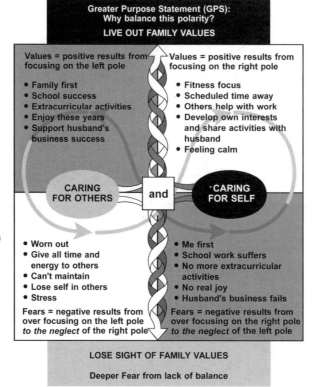

Action Steps

How will we gain or maintain the positive results from focusing on this left pole? What? Who? By when? Measures?

Early Warnings

Measurable indicators (things you can count) that will let you know that you are getting into the downside of this left pole.

1. Avg. <7 hrs. sleep per night.
2. Sun <30 min., 3 days per week.
3. Jack available <2 hrs. school nights Tues. thru Thurs.
4. Point system.

Greater Purpose Statement (GPS): Why balance this polarity? LIVE OUT FAMILY VALUES

Values = positive results from focusing on the left pole

- Family first
- School success
- Extracurricular activities
- Enjoy these years
- Support husband's business success

Values = positive results from focusing on the right pole

- Fitness focus
- Scheduled time away
- Others help with work
- Develop own interests and share activities with husband
- Feeling calm

CARING FOR OTHERS and **CARING FOR SELF**

- Worn out
- Give all time and energy to others
- Can't maintain
- Lose self in others
- Stress

Fears = negative results from over focusing on the left pole *to the neglect of the right pole*

- Me first
- School work suffers
- No more extracurricular activities
- No real joy
- Husband's business fails

Fears = negative results from over focusing on the right pole *to the neglect of the left pole*

LOSE SIGHT OF FAMILY VALUES

Deeper Fear from lack of balance

Action Steps

How will we gain or maintain the positive results from focusing on this right pole? What? Who? By when? Measures?

1. 7 hrs. sleep each night.
2. Exercise 4 times per week.
3. Re-enlist Jack's help.
4. Manage point system.
5. 1 night out per month.
6. 2 date nights per month.

Early Warnings

Measurable indicators (things you can count) that will let you know that you are getting into the downside of this right pole.

1. Homework incomplete.
2. Missed music and dance lessons.
3. Bad feelings about 1 and 2.
4. Jack misses important business deadlines.
5. Not able to help Jack when he needs it.

Polarity Map #10

Lisa kept talking, "And, the Action Steps I need to focus on to maintain positive results for Caring for Others, but not to the neglect of Caring for Self," she said with a smile, "would be to check homework every night and get the girls

Action Steps to refocus on Caring for Others

to their lessons on time. That will make us all happy. Oh, and I have to support Jack and his business and be ready to help when he needs me."

I wrote in these final thoughts and again turned the map for Lisa to see.

Action Steps

How will we gain or maintain the positive results from focusing on this left pole? What? Who? By when? Measures?

1. Check homework every night.
2. Girls arrive on time for music and dance.
3. Support Jack and business.
4. Be available to help.

Early Warnings

Measurable indicators (things you can count) that will let you know that you are getting into the downside of this left pole.

1. Avg. <7 hrs. sleep per night.
2. Sun <30 min., 3 days per week.
3. Jack available <2 hrs. school nights Tues. thru Thurs.
4. Point system.

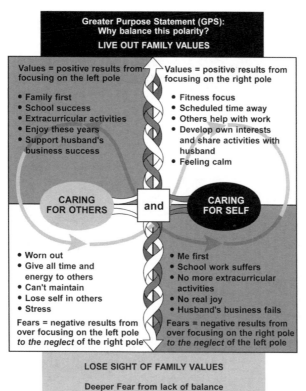

Greater Purpose Statement (GPS): Why balance this polarity?
LIVE OUT FAMILY VALUES

Values = positive results from focusing on the left pole

Values = positive results from focusing on the right pole

- Family first
- School success
- Extracurricular activities
- Enjoy these years
- Support husband's business success

- Fitness focus
- Scheduled time away
- Others help with work
- Develop own interests and share activities with husband
- Feeling calm

CARING FOR OTHERS and **CARING FOR SELF**

- Worn out
- Give all time and energy to others
- Can't maintain
- Lose self in others
- Stress

- Me first
- School work suffers
- No more extracurricular activities
- No real joy
- Husband's business fails

Fears = negative results from over focusing on the left pole *to the neglect of the right pole*

Fears = negative results from over focusing on the right pole *to the neglect of the left pole*

LOSE SIGHT OF FAMILY VALUES

Deeper Fear from lack of balance

Action Steps

How will we gain or maintain the positive results from focusing on this right pole? What? Who? By when? Measures?

1. 7 hrs. sleep each night.
2. Exercise 4 times per week.
3. Re-enlist Jack's help.
4. Manage point system.
5. 1 night out per month.
6. 2 date nights per month.

Early Warnings

Measurable indicators (things you can count) that will let you know that you are getting into the downside of this right pole.

1. Homework incomplete.
2. Missed music and dance lessons.
3. Bad feelings about 1 and 2.
4. Jack misses important business deadlines.
5. Not able to help Jack when he needs it.

Polarity Map #11

"I can see it so clearly now!" Lisa exclaimed. "In order to maintain a balanced, family-centered home, I need to care for others and care for myself, and the best way to do that is to focus on these Action Steps and Early Warnings. Action Steps and Early Warnings are the keys to balance. The answer seems so simple laid out on the Polarity Map.

"I'm really glad this has helped, Lisa—you've really uncovered a lot here today!" I said smiling.

Lisa replied, "Yes, this has been great, coach. I want to title this map My Balanced, Family-Centered Home." Lisa wrote in her title on the top of the map.

Name the Map

My Balanced, Family-Centered Home

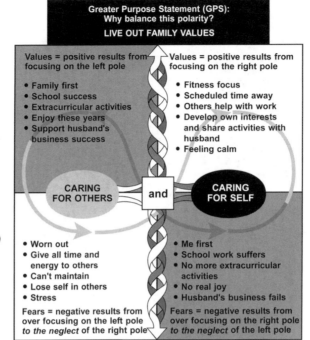

Action Steps

How will we gain or maintain the positive results from focusing on this left pole? What? Who? By when? Measures?

1. Check homework every night.
2. Girls arrive on time for music and dance.
3. Support Jack and business.
4. Be available to help.

Greater Purpose Statement (GPS): Why balance this polarity?
LIVE OUT FAMILY VALUES

Values = positive results from focusing on the left pole

- Family first
- School success
- Extracurricular activities
- Enjoy these years
- Support husband's business success

Values = positive results from focusing on the right pole

- Fitness focus
- Scheduled time away
- Others help with work
- Develop own interests and share activities with husband
- Feeling calm

CARING FOR OTHERS **and** CARING FOR SELF

- Worn out
- Give all time and energy to others
- Can't maintain
- Lose self in others
- Stress

Fears = negative results from over focusing on the left pole *to the neglect* of the right pole

- Me first
- School work suffers
- No more extracurricular activities
- No real joy
- Husband's business fails

Fears = negative results from over focusing on the right pole *to the neglect* of the left pole

LOSE SIGHT OF FAMILY VALUES

Deeper Fear from lack of balance

Action Steps

How will we gain or maintain the positive results from focusing on this right pole? What? Who? By when? Measures?

1. 7 hrs. sleep each night.
2. Exercise 4 times per week.
3. Re-enlist Jack's help.
4. Manage point system.
5. 1 night out per month.
6. 2 date nights per month.

Early Warnings

Measurable indicators (things you can count) that will let you know that you are getting into the downside of this left pole.

1. Avg. <7 hrs. sleep per night.
2. Sun <30 min., 3 days per week.
3. Jack available <2 hrs. school nights Tues. thru Thurs.
4. Point system.

Early Warnings

Measurable indicators (things you can count) that will let you know that you are getting into the downside of this right pole.

1. Homework incomplete.
2. Missed music and dance lessons.
3. Bad feelings about 1 and 2.
4. Jack misses important business deadlines.
5. Not able to help Jack when he needs it.

Polarity Map #12

"So between now and next week, what step or steps do you want to take to move this forward?" I asked.

"Yes, this is where I have to begin taking action, and my first step will be to share this with Jack. We can learn together through this process. And my goal is to have at least one of these Action Steps in place by the time we meet next week." Lisa paused and smiled, "You know, I wasn't quite sure what to expect from our coaching today—this has been so helpful! Thank you, Kathy!"

~

This case is a great example of the opportunity the client had to live a more balanced life. Polarity Coaching is a process that can help a client understand that when the full picture of the polarity to manage is in view, intentional behavior that utilizes Action Steps and Early Warnings will maintain the balance of the polarity—in this case caring for self and caring for others—in sync.

~

In the next case, we are reminded of a very well-known saying, "opposites attract." Polarity Management is helpful in seeking to understand what another person, in this case Annie, may be thinking and feeling. As the real difficulty is uncovered, Matt experiences how Polarity Coaching opens the way to both understand and appreciate what initially appears to be opposing positions.

Case Study #3
Planned and Spontaneous

Matt and Annie had been married nearly 10 years, and as they approached their 10-year wedding anniversary, they began talking about how they would celebrate. They agreed on a Florida vacation—a vacation they both wanted to remember for years to come. Matt could not wait to begin planning each day of their vacation and decide where they would go, what they would do, and how it would fit into the budget. Annie saw things differently. She longed for two weeks of freedom and wanted to do whatever came their way—scheduling their flight and their car was all the planning she needed. They had not been on a nice vacation in years, and although she was aware they had a budget, she also felt this was a time they could splurge. As much as they tried to share their feelings, their conversations had come to an impasse, and the tension was about to burst the bubble of their dream vacation for both of them. Matt talked with his sister about the tension both he and Annie were experiencing. Matt's sister recommended that he call a coach.

Having established our coaching relationship, Matt began to tell me the merits of carefully planning their vacation. "We've waited a long time to go on a nice vacation, and these two weeks are important to both of us," he explained. "We need to plan ahead, or the vacation could become a disaster."

"What do you see as the problem?" I prompted.

Matt answered, "I've tried to help Annie see the importance of planning this vacation, but each time I try to explain, we hit a wall. She just doesn't seem to understand. Maybe I should just quit trying, but I'm afraid our time will be wasted and that we'll spend more than we can afford. I'm stuck, and I need to know what I should do."

"Matt, you have an important goal you want to reach. You have a vision of an ideal vacation, celebrating your 10th wedding anniversary," I affirmed.

"Yes, that's right," Matt answered.

"As your coach, I will embrace that goal with you. I will listen to you, challenge you, encourage you, use my intuition, and bring a fresh viewpoint. However, I can't tell you what to do. That must come from you and perhaps from Annie. While we are coaching, you must own this issue, and I will hold you accountable to move forward on your goal. It will be your job to explore the situation at a deeper level and take action to move ahead," I explained.

"I understand," said Matt, nodding in agreement.

"To get started, I'd like to ask you a few questions. First, tell me what is it that you are hoping for?" I asked.

"I'm hoping that Annie and I can sit down and plan a memorable 10-year anniversary vacation, what we are going to do, where to stay, and how much money we will spend," Matt answered.

"And Annie, what is she hoping for?" I asked.

"I think Annie wants a memorable vacation too, but she doesn't want to plan anything. Sure, we've had conversations about going to a theme park and spending a few days at the beach, but that's as far as we get. When I try to nail something down, she resists," Matt sighed.

"Let me ask you, Matt, have you and Annie dealt with this kind of challenge in the past?" I inquired.

"Yes, we have," Matt answered, eager to respond. "I knew before we were married that Annie tended to do things on the spur-of-the-moment. When we met, she was in college, and I would always wonder why she would put off doing homework. I would be the one worrying, and she would be fine, and then she would burn the midnight oil as she tried to finish a paper. Somehow she was always able to get things done, but I couldn't understand why she'd put herself through that last-minute stress. I am the opposite—I prefer scheduling, and I manage things in a more planful way."

Matt continued, "There are other examples. I like to plan within our budget, while Annie can be comfortable making big purchasing decisions sometimes without thinking things through if it's something she really wants. We've both had to compromise on this over the years; I know Annie can see the big picture, and she appreciates that I am cautious about our budget," Matt said proudly.

"Grocery shopping is another example. Of course I prefer to have my list with me, while she'll walk down the aisles of the grocery store and put things into the cart from off the top of her head!" He added, "She has had to make a second trip back to the store many times because something we needed was forgotten, but this doesn't seem to bother her. I'm more relaxed about this than I used to be because I can see that it usually works out."

"When it comes to the kids, I'm the stricter disciplinarian, while she will let the kids explore and learn on their own. I appreciate this balance for the kids, and I know it is good for them, too." Matt paused to reflect and then continued, "Annie has actually begun planning more since the kids started school. She will lay out their clothes the night before and make sure the back packs are ready to go so that the mornings aren't so hectic. I'm all in favor of that, and it teaches the kids to be organized."

"It sounds like there may be wisdom in the resistance. As we coach, Matt, see if you are able to move toward the resistance, rather than away from it. What I mean by that is that Annie values planning in some instances, and you have been able to relax a little when Annie is more laid back or spontaneous," I said. Then to clarify, I asked, "Is *spontaneous* the right word to describe Annie?"

"Definitely, she's spontaneous, and sometimes I love that about her" Matt agreed. "It has helped me relax more about some things. I can see that sometimes

I'm too inflexible, which Annie tends to point out from time-to-time," Matt added with a blush.

"What I think I'm hearing is that both of you recognize each other's preferred pattern of behavior: you are more on the planning side and Annie more naturally spontaneous," I said, trying to distill down what Matt had said.

"Yes, I would agree with that," Matt responded.

"It also sounds like you've been able to accept your differences," I said to confirm, "and as you've experienced each other's natural tendencies, you have even grown to appreciate and engage each other's natural tendencies as your own from time-to-time."

"Yes, I believe that's true," Matt said reflecting on what was being said.

"So Matt, tell me what is getting in the way now?" I asked.

Matt started slowly, "I feel we need to plan our vacation carefully. I try to explain this to Annie, but every time I talk about it, Annie resists even more, and we don't get anywhere. This is taking all the fun out of planning, and the clearer I communicate my point of view, the more Annie resists. Like I said, I'm stuck!"

"Matt, what might the spontaneous part of you say?" I asked.

"I don't understand," Matt answered.

"I heard you say that Annie is naturally drawn toward the spontaneous part of her—it's what I would call her natural tendency, or motivational value. And she also sees the value of planning, what I would call your natural tendency or motivational value. I also heard you say that even as a natural planner, you can see the value of being spontaneous from time-to-time," I responded.

"Yes, that's true," Matt replied.

"Tell me then, what might the spontaneous part of you say about your vacation?" I repeated.

Matt hesitated, "I guess I'm not looking at this from a spontaneous point of view. I've been focused on the planning part of the vacation," Matt answered thoughtfully.

"What perspective do you think Annie is looking at this vacation from, Matt: planned or spontaneous?" I questioned.

"I know it's not from a planning perspective!" Matt said confidently.

"Do you think this is to be expected?" I continued.

"Yes, you're right; I should expect this," Matt answered with a sigh.

"Matt, do you see how Annie might resist a process of planning your vacation that does not include spontaneity?" I asked.

"Yes, I can see that now," Matt answered keenly.

I continued, "What I believe this is, Matt, is a polarity to manage, not a problem to solve. "

"A polarity to manage?" Matt questioned with a puzzled look.

"Yes", I answered. "Let me explain. Deciding where to go on your vacation is a problem to solve, and you have both agreed on Florida. You basically made a decision and you moved on. A polarity to manage is different, and when a polarity to manage is treated as a decision to be made, resistance occurs. With a polarity to manage, both points of view are accurate, and neither is complete in and of itself. In fact, both points of view are dependant on one another for a successful outcome," I paused as Matt thought this through.

"I think I understand what you are saying," Matt stated somewhat apprehensively.

"What polarities do you think are at work here, Matt?" I asked.

"Well, I'm not sure," Matt hesitated. "But we've been talking a lot about planning and being spontaneous—would the polarities be planned and spontaneous?"

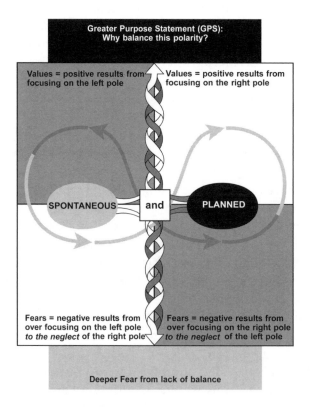

"Yes," I continued, excited that Matt could see this. "I think the polarity to manage is planned and spontaneous, and focusing on either one and neglecting the other brings resistance."

"This sounds interesting," Matt said. "I've been experiencing resistance, please continue."

"Let me draw you a map," I offered. "Here's what I've heard so far."

I drew a Polarity Map™, filled in the poles with Planned and Spontaneous, and shared it with Matt.

Name the Poles

Greater Purpose Statement (GPS):
Why balance this polarity?

Values = positive results from focusing on the left pole

Values = positive results from focusing on the right pole

SPONTANEOUS   and   PLANNED

Fears = negative results from over focusing on the left pole *to the neglect* of the right pole

Fears = negative results from over focusing on the right pole *to the neglect* of the left pole

Deeper Fear from lack of balance

Polarity Map #1

"The top box, called the Greater Purpose, is what you want to achieve; it's your goal. I think that could be a memorable Florida vacation. Does that sound right?" I asked.

Greater Purpose

"Yes, that's what this is all about," Matt confirmed.

"And the bottom box is what you want to avoid, the Deeper Fear—what would go into the bottom box?" I asked.

"That would be a miserable Florida vacation," Matt answered. "I want to avoid a miserable Florida vacation.

Deeper Fear

I wrote in the Greater Purpose and Deeper Fear.

"Now let's look at the two ovals," I continued as I pointed to them on the map. "The two ovals are called interdependent poles. The interdependent poles are Planned and Spontaneous. Planned and Spontaneous both contain the positive aspects you've talked about. They both have an upside or place to list the values of each pole," I said as I pointed to the upper quadrants. "And they both contain negative results, which is called the downside or place to list the negative aspects of each pole," I continued as I pointed to the lower quadrants.

"I can see that," said Matt as he seemed to reflect on our earlier conversation.

"Here's another important part of the map," I said as I drew Matt's attention to the spiraling arrows. "The downward spiraling synergy arrows show the potential for the tension between the two poles to negatively reinforce each other, moving the polarity toward the Deeper Fear, or in this case, a miserable Florida vacation."

"That's where we are," Matt said curiously, "I think we are spiraling downward."

Virtuous and Vicious Cycles

"And, the upward spiraling synergy arrows show the potential for the tension between the two poles to positively reinforce each other, moving the polarity toward the Greater Purpose, a memorable Florida vacation.

"That's where I want to be," Matt said firmly.

"And finally, the Infinity Loop," I said as I traced the flow of the Infinity Loop across the map. "This shows how a polarity to manage oscillates from one pole to the other. It is possible to manage a

Infinity Loop

polarity well, gain positive results of both upsides, and move up toward the Greater Purpose while minimizing the effects of both downsides," I assured Matt as he studied the map.

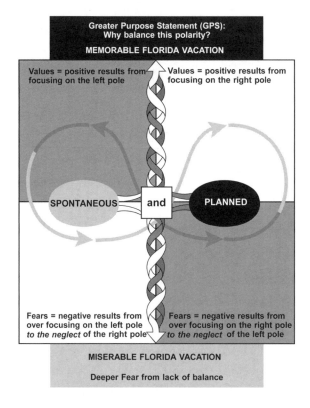

Polarity Map #2

"Shall we fill in the quadrants?" I asked.

"Let's try it," Matt agreed.

"Okay. Let me ask you this, Matt: what about spontaneity works for you?" I asked.

Pausing a moment, Matt began, "I have to be honest here. I know that I can be rigid at times, and Annie is much more flexible than I am. I can see it when something unexpected comes up, Annie handles this with ease. Whether it's in our family or if someone calls and needs her help, she doesn't hesitate to help if she can, in fact, she will just drop what she's doing and respond to the situation. I really admire that about her. I have tried to be more like her in that way and be more flexible at times when the unexpected happens."

"Wow! That's great!" I acknowledged. "What else?"

Matt replied, "As I said, Annie will give the boys more freedom and independence than I would typically allow, and I can see this has been a positive influence in their lives. I think it has **Upper Left Quadrant for Spontaneous** helped them to become good decision makers. I have also learned to lighten up and have tried to change in that way."

"Can you say more about that?" I asked.

"I find myself making the same decisions over and over, going to the same restaurant, making the same choices, spending my free time the same way. I have comfortable patterns, which isn't all bad, but Annie has helped me be aware of the choices I have in life. She would say, 'Matt, you have a rich life; you have choices!' Her encouragement has helped me start looking at various choices and knowing I can experience something new and different, so I'm working on that, and Annie loves it," Matt answered, his face lighting up as he responded.

"Okay, so I heard you mention flexibility, freedom and independence, choices, and feeling energized as positive values in the spontaneous pole," I said. "I have written them here on the map," I added as I turned the map for Matt to see.

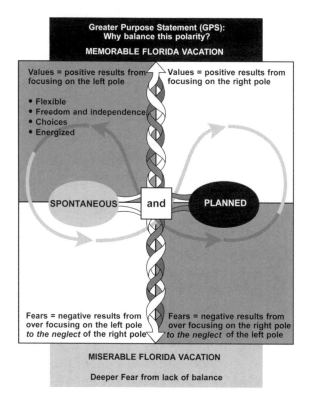

Polarity Map #3

"Yes, I agree that I value those aspects of spontaneity," Matt said.

"And what do you think Annie appreciates about spontaneity?" I asked.

"Annie would appreciate all those same things—and she loves to wake up and discover each day as a new adventure," Matt said smiling.

"Shall we add that to the map?" I asked.

"Definitely," Matt replied.

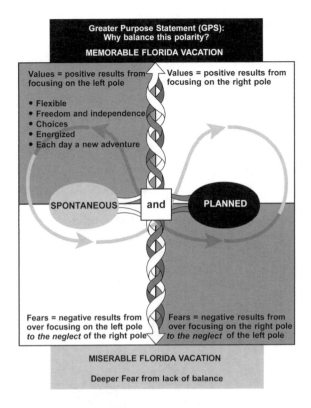

Polarity Map #4

"Next, Matt, what do you fear about spontaneity?" I asked.

"That's easy," Matt answered quickly.
"Especially on important issues, I need to be
clear, to understand what's going on, and to
know what to expect. Annie is comfortable with

> **Lower Left Quadrant
> for Spontaneous**

ambiguity, but I'm not. It drives me crazy when she doesn't communicate
clearly; she starts talking before she has really thought things through. She will
jump from one perspective to another, and sometimes she's so vague I don't
even know where she stands or what she wants."

I wrote "Ambiguous" and "Vague" on the map.

"All that I can deal with," Matt continued, "That is what is most important
to me is managing the spontaneity, if that makes sense. What I mean is, I want to
have realistic expectations, and I like to look at the pros and cons and make sure
we have some control over the outcome. I'm not a risk taker. I gauge things and
avoid foolish risks and waste, whether it's time or money I don't like to waste it."
Matt concluded.

"And for Annie, is there a downside to spontaneity?" I asked.

Matt answered, "I think she would agree, especially now that we are older
and with the kids, that we can't make big financial mistakes—we don't have as
many years to recover from them."

"So how would Annie describe that?" I asked.

"I think she would say that there could be potential for a costly penalty if we were being too spontaneous with bigger decisions, like buying a new car before we were really able to afford it."

I wrote the main themes on the map and gave it to Matt.

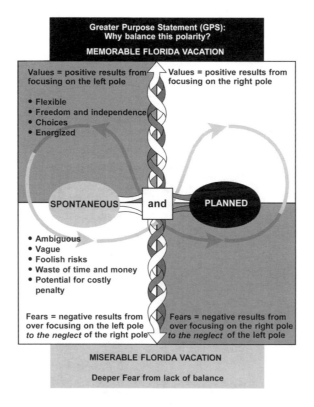

Polarity Map #5

"Yes, that looks good, that's the downside of Spontaneous," Matt said.

"Okay, Matt, let's look at Planned. What about Planned do you think works for Annie?" I asked.

"Wow—that's a good question. I know what works for me, but I'm not too sure about Annie," Matt said. He thought a moment and then continued thoughtfully, "I know Annie likes the fact that I am grounded about things. She has often told me that she appreciates knowing where I stand on important decisions we have to make. It sets the stage for a common understanding, especially with the boys, and I think she values that. I feel Annie also appreciates how I plan our finances, and she

Upper Right Quadrant for Planned

has told me that she feels a sense of security that I am looking ahead at our future. We have discussed our future goals, and keeping our future goals in mind and reaching those goals are important to both of us."

"Okay, I'm hearing four things that represent the upside of Planned: clarity, common understanding, security, and reaching future goals," I said. "And are you in sync with those?" I asked.

"Yes, absolutely," Matt answered.

"Would you add anything to this list, Matt?" I asked.

Matt once again thought carefully about my question.

"I guess I like the fact that for the most part, there won't be any big surprises. Surprises may be unavoidable in some cases, but an upside of planning means we have a contingency for those things we can plan for," Matt responded.

"So if you boiled that down to a few words, what would that be?" I asked.

"Contingency plans," Matt said quickly.

"Okay, I'm adding those five things to the upside of Planned," I responded as I turned the map to share with Matt again.

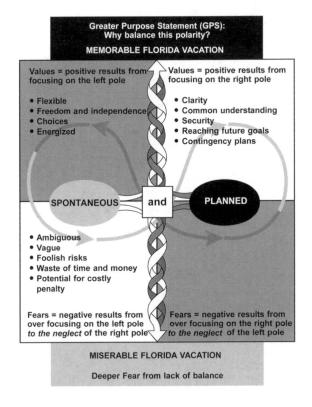

Polarity Map #6

Matt looked at the map and nodded in agreement and turned the map back for me to continue.

"And what does Annie fear about this pole; what do you think is the downside of Planned for her?" I asked.

Matt answered, "Well, I know that Annie thinks I can be too rigid and inflexible. She enjoys the freedom and independence of spontaneity, and for her the downside of planning is probably setting boundaries and restrictions."

> **Lower Right Quadrant for Planned**

Matt thought for a moment, and then continued, "I think this would include a feeling of lost opportunities to try new things when she feels things are planned too tightly. She might also feel bored because she really does love to be free to try new things."

"Okay, I have that. Is there anything you would add from your perspective, Matt?" I asked.

"That's a hard question for me," said Matt as he paused. "All I can think of is that when I'm being more spontaneous, I'm stretching myself, and sometimes it's kind of fun. So I guess a downside of Planned would be that my life would be too rote, you know, too monotonous—life would be too monotonous."

I finished the last quadrant and turned the map to Matt.

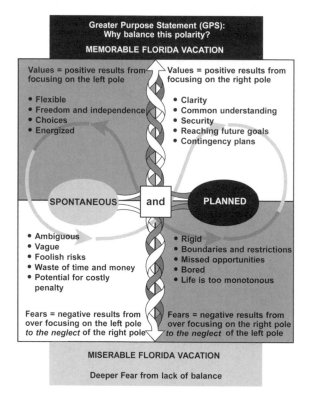

Polarity Map #7

"Matt, what do you see on this map?" I asked.

49

Matt was serious. "When it comes to this vacation, I think Annie is seeing the downside of Planned. She probably sees me as too rigid, and feels I'm putting boundaries and restrictions around this vacation. She's probably concerned that she won't get to do all the things she wants to do, and she won't have as much fun as she could have. This map makes it pretty clear."

"Sounds feasible, Matt," I affirmed. "So what do you think needs to happen?"

"I need to follow the Infinity Loop to the upside of Spontaneous," Matt answered. "I guess I should be more flexible, be a little freer so that Annie can have more choices to make on the fly. I think she'd be happier if we have some adventure while we are away, and we will have a more memorable Florida vacation."

"Can you do that, Matt?" I asked.

Matt was cautious. "Yes, but I still have to watch our spending, and we have to plan some things ahead of time."

"Sure, it's about balance!" I acknowledged. "If there wasn't any planning, the downside of Spontaneous would become reality, and you'd be on that spiral down to a miserable vacation."

"Yes, I see that. We have to be spontaneous as well as plan in order to have a memorable Florida vacation. But how do we experience both the upside of Planned and Spontaneous?" Matt asked. "How do we achieve the balance we are talking about?"

"This is where Action Steps and Early Warnings come in," I answered as I drew Action Steps and Early Warnings onto the map.

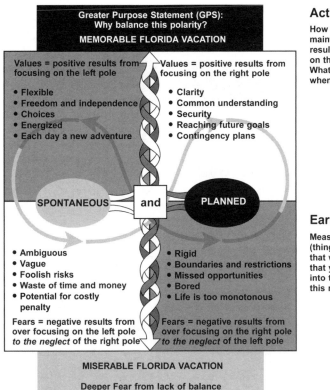

Action Steps

How will we gain or maintain the positive results from focusing on this left pole? What? Who? By when? Measures?

Greater Purpose Statement (GPS): Why balance this polarity?
MEMORABLE FLORIDA VACATION

Values = positive results from focusing on the left pole

- Flexible
- Freedom and independence
- Choices
- Energized
- Each day a new adventure

Values = positive results from focusing on the right pole

- Clarity
- Common understanding
- Security
- Reaching future goals
- Contingency plans

SPONTANEOUS and **PLANNED**

Action Steps

How will we gain or maintain the positive results from focusing on this right pole? What? Who? By when? Measures?

Early Warnings

Measurable indicators (things you can count) that will let you know that you are getting into the downside of this left pole.

- Ambiguous
- Vague
- Foolish risks
- Waste of time and money
- Potential for costly penalty

Fears = negative results from over focusing on the left pole *to the neglect* of the right pole

- Rigid
- Boundaries and restrictions
- Missed opportunities
- Bored
- Life is too monotonous

Fears = negative results from over focusing on the right pole *to the neglect* of the left pole

Early Warnings

Measurable indicators (things you can count) that will let you know that you are getting into the downside of this right pole.

MISERABLE FLORIDA VACATION

Deeper Fear from lack of balance

Polarity Map #8

"The Action Steps and Early Warnings help you see and sustain balance between the interdependent poles of Planned and Spontaneous. Let me explain what I mean," I continued. "Annie may experience positive results of Spontaneous if she knows there is free time on the schedule."

"Oh, I get it! I should plan in time to be spontaneous," Matt clarified.

"Yes. You could do that," I agreed.

"Okay, and I could plan how much money to have in the spontaneous budget for spontaneous shopping," Matt winked.

"Yes, you could do that, too," I responded. "Do you think Annie would see that as positive steps that would meet her need to bring spontaneous time and spontaneous spending into your vacation?" I asked.

> **Action Steps to refocus on Spontaneous**

"I think so," Matt said thoughtfully. "And she would probably like it if out of the blue I suggested something like a special dinner, or if I surprised her and took her somewhere to dance one night."

"Wow, that sounds like a nice surprise!" I said supportively as I wrote in the Spontaneous Action Steps Matt had identified.

I turned the map for Matt to see.

"Yes," Matt said as he read the map. "I think this will work for Annie, and I know it will work for me."

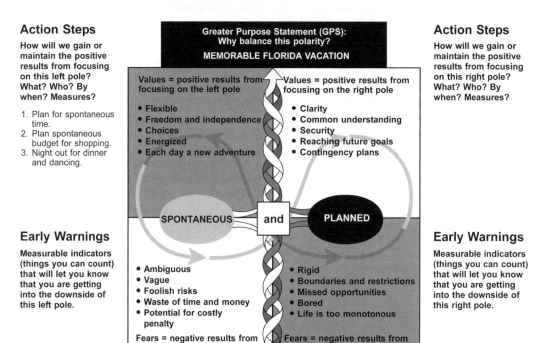

Action Steps

How will we gain or maintain the positive results from focusing on this left pole? What? Who? By when? Measures?

1. Plan for spontaneous time.
2. Plan spontaneous budget for shopping.
3. Night out for dinner and dancing.

Action Steps

How will we gain or maintain the positive results from focusing on this right pole? What? Who? By when? Measures?

Greater Purpose Statement (GPS): Why balance this polarity?
MEMORABLE FLORIDA VACATION

Values = positive results from focusing on the left pole

- Flexible
- Freedom and independence
- Choices
- Energized
- Each day a new adventure

Values = positive results from focusing on the right pole

- Clarity
- Common understanding
- Security
- Reaching future goals
- Contingency plans

SPONTANEOUS and **PLANNED**

- Ambiguous
- Vague
- Foolish risks
- Waste of time and money
- Potential for costly penalty

- Rigid
- Boundaries and restrictions
- Missed opportunities
- Bored
- Life is too monotonous

Fears = negative results from over focusing on the left pole *to the neglect* of the right pole

Fears = negative results from over focusing on the right pole *to the neglect* of the left pole

MISERABLE FLORIDA VACATION

Deeper Fear from lack of balance

Early Warnings

Measurable indicators (things you can count) that will let you know that you are getting into the downside of this left pole.

Early Warnings

Measurable indicators (things you can count) that will let you know that you are getting into the downside of this right pole.

Polarity Map #9

Matt began again, "Now the downside of Spontaneous. I'm concerned that when we over focus on Spontaneous, we will miss something important, something we both really want to do. And I predict that when we are doing unplanned activities, we will overspend. It's funny because even before that happens, I know I will start getting tense. I guess if I'm not reviewing the budget, I anticipate the downside of Spontaneous even before we get there."

"Okay. So Early Warnings could be a tense feeling and overspending," I said as I started to fill in the Early Warnings.

> **Early Warnings due to an over focus on Spontaneous**

"Yes, and missing out on something we don't want to miss out on," Matt repeated.

"Oh, yes," I said as I continued writing.

I turned the map for Matt to see. "What do you think?" I asked Matt.

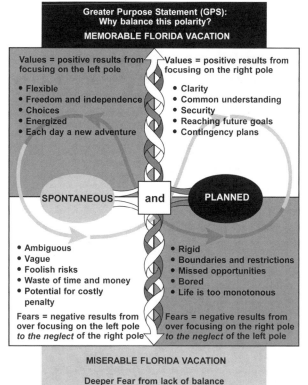

Action Steps

How will we gain or maintain the positive results from focusing on this left pole? What? Who? By when? Measures?

1. Plan for spontaneous time.
2. Plan spontaneous budget for shopping.
3. Night out for dinner and dancing.

Early Warnings

Measurable indicators (things you can count) that will let you know that you are getting into the downside of this left pole.

1. Tense feeling.
2. Budget is overspent.
3. Missed important event.

Greater Purpose Statement (GPS): Why balance this polarity?
MEMORABLE FLORIDA VACATION

Values = positive results from focusing on the left pole

- Flexible
- Freedom and independence
- Choices
- Energized
- Each day a new adventure

Values = positive results from focusing on the right pole

- Clarity
- Common understanding
- Security
- Reaching future goals
- Contingency plans

SPONTANEOUS and PLANNED

- Ambiguous
- Vague
- Foolish risks
- Waste of time and money
- Potential for costly penalty

Fears = negative results from over focusing on the left pole *to the neglect* of the right pole

- Rigid
- Boundaries and restrictions
- Missed opportunities
- Bored
- Life is too monotonous

Fears = negative results from over focusing on the right pole *to the neglect* of the left pole

MISERABLE FLORIDA VACATION

Deeper Fear from lack of balance

Action Steps

How will we gain or maintain the positive results from focusing on this right pole? What? Who? By when? Measures?

Early Warnings

Measurable indicators (things you can count) that will let you know that you are getting into the downside of this right pole.

Polarity Map #10

"Yes, that looks good, and this might sound silly, but as long as I plan in the spontaneous time and spontaneous budget, I don't think I'll feel tense. It won't feel like the downside of Spontaneous to me," Matt said pointing to the downside of Spontaneous. "And Annie won't see me as rigid or boring," he added as he moved his finger across the map to the downside of Planned.

"That is great!" I said in support.

"Yes, that is a gift I hadn't expected," Matt said earnestly. "Thank you, Coach!"

"I'm glad you are pleased, Matt." I said sincerely.

"There are two more parts of the map," I continued, "the Action Steps and Early Warnings for Planned. What are the Action Steps needed in order to experience the upside of Planned?" I asked.

"It would be to do the important things we agreed we really wanted to do while we are on vacation," Matt answered, "and I think it would be to review the budget, and to plan exceptions together."

> **Action Steps to refocus on Planned**

"Got it," I responded as I wrote in what Matt had said.

Turning the map again so that Matt could take a look, he nodded in agreement.

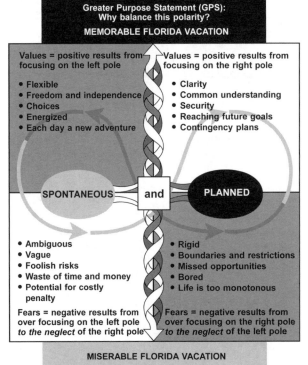

Action Steps

How will we gain or maintain the positive results from focusing on this left pole? What? Who? By when? Measures?

1. Plan for spontaneous time.
2. Plan spontaneous budget for shopping.
3. Night out for dinner and dancing.

Action Steps

How will we gain or maintain the positive results from focusing on this right pole? What? Who? By when? Measures?

1. Review the budget.
2. Plan exceptions together.
3. Do the important things you both enjoy.

Greater Purpose Statement (GPS): Why balance this polarity? MEMORABLE FLORIDA VACATION

Values = positive results from focusing on the left pole

- Flexible
- Freedom and independence
- Choices
- Energized
- Each day a new adventure

Values = positive results from focusing on the right pole

- Clarity
- Common understanding
- Security
- Reaching future goals
- Contingency plans

SPONTANEOUS and **PLANNED**

- Ambiguous
- Vague
- Foolish risks
- Waste of time and money
- Potential for costly penalty

Fears = negative results from over focusing on the left pole *to the neglect* of the right pole

- Rigid
- Boundaries and restrictions
- Missed opportunities
- Bored
- Life is too monotonous

Fears = negative results from over focusing on the right pole *to the neglect* of the left pole

MISERABLE FLORIDA VACATION

Deeper Fear from lack of balance

Early Warnings

Measurable indicators (things you can count) that will let you know that you are getting into the downside of this left pole.

1. Tense feeling.
2. Budget is overspent.
3. Missed important event.

Early Warnings

Measurable indicators (things you can count) that will let you know that you are getting into the downside of this right pole.

Polarity Map #11

"Finally, Matt, tell me how will you know if you are experiencing the downside of Planned?" I asked.

Matt smiled. "For me, I don't see a downside, but for Annie—I know her—Annie will buy a magazine. Yes, I know her well," Matt said and smiled again. "When she gets bored she picks up a magazine and reads stories about other people's lives. And then she'll start reading them to me!"

> **Early Warnings due to an over focus on Planned**

"Okay. So an Early Warning that Annie is experiencing the downside of Planned is the magazine, and she'll communicate it by reading the magazine to you," I repeated.

"Yes, and she won't tell me that she is bored," Matt added. "She'll say something like 'How long do you want to watch the paint dry, Honey?'"

"That's funny," I said smiling. "So you know Annie is bored and experiencing the downside of Planned when she hints to you with a comment in jest?"

"In jest, yes," Matt answered candidly, "but I know how she's really feeling. So I guess you could say I experience the downside, too."

I wrote, "Annie buys magazines," "Reads magazine to Matt," and "Watch the paint dry," in the Early Warnings of the downside of Planned.

I turned the map so that Matt could look at the finished product.

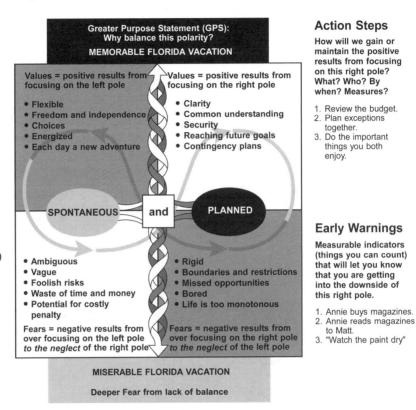

Action Steps

How will we gain or maintain the positive results from focusing on this left pole? What? Who? By when? Measures?

1. Plan for spontaneous time.
2. Plan spontaneous budget for shopping.
3. Night out for dinner and dancing.

Action Steps

How will we gain or maintain the positive results from focusing on this right pole? What? Who? By when? Measures?

1. Review the budget.
2. Plan exceptions together.
3. Do the important things you both enjoy.

Early Warnings

Measurable indicators (things you can count) that will let you know that you are getting into the downside of this left pole.

1. Tense feeling.
2. Budget is overspent.
3. Missed important event.

Early Warnings

Measurable indicators (things you can count) that will let you know that you are getting into the downside of this right pole.

1. Annie buys magazines.
2. Annie reads magazines to Matt.
3. "Watch the paint dry"

Greater Purpose Statement (GPS): Why balance this polarity?
MEMORABLE FLORIDA VACATION

Values = positive results from focusing on the left pole
- Flexible
- Freedom and independence
- Choices
- Energized
- Each day a new adventure

Values = positive results from focusing on the right pole
- Clarity
- Common understanding
- Security
- Reaching future goals
- Contingency plans

SPONTANEOUS **and** PLANNED

- Ambiguous
- Vague
- Foolish risks
- Waste of time and money
- Potential for costly penalty

Fears = negative results from over focusing on the left pole *to the neglect* of the right pole

- Rigid
- Boundaries and restrictions
- Missed opportunities
- Bored
- Life is too monotonous

Fears = negative results from over focusing on the right pole *to the neglect* of the left pole

MISERABLE FLORIDA VACATION

Deeper Fear from lack of balance

Polarity Map #12

Matt studied the Polarity Map.

"What's your next step, Matt?" I asked.

"Well, coach," Matt answered. "When we started this conversation, I thought you would give me ideas on how to convince Annie that we needed to carefully plan the vacation. Actually," Matt hesitated momentarily and then continued, "you have helped me do that, and now I know that there is a need to plan for spontaneity as well. Does that make sense?" Matt questioned.

"Yes, Matt, it does!" I affirmed.

Matt continued, "We were in a power struggle. I see now that if I had insisted on planning each step of this vacation like I wanted to, Annie would not have enjoyed our vacation. In the same way, if I gave up and nothing was planned, I wouldn't have been able to enjoy the vacation; either way we would spiral down to a miserable vacation. I had no idea I was stuck in a polarity."

"You have a good understanding of Polarity Management, Matt!" I exclaimed.

"What's next?" I asked.

"What's next?" Matt repeated. "First, I want to share this with Annie. By showing her our natural tendencies toward spontaneity and planning and explaining how we can balance those natural tendencies, we will have the best spontaneously planned 10-year anniversary vacation we can possibly have!" Matt said confidently. "I also think there is an opportunity for Annie and me to use Polarity Management in other areas such as our finances and parenting perhaps. It would be great to explore some of that with you when we get back."

"Of course, Matt," I answered. "Polarity Management helps us see and understand how our natural tendencies are unique to each of us as individuals and how they influence our lives. The Polarity Map illustrates how to successfully manage the tension between those tendencies over time."

We concluded our session with a commitment to coach again in one month.

"Thank you, coach!" Matt said confidently as he wrote "A Great Two-Week Vacation" on the top of the map and turned it for me to see.

Name the Map

A Great Two-Week Vacation!

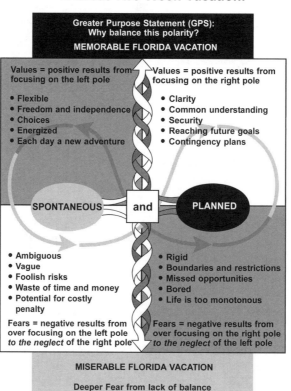

Action Steps

How will we gain or maintain the positive results from focusing on this left pole? What? Who? By when? Measures?

1. Plan for spontaneous time.
2. Plan spontaneous budget for shopping.
3. Night out for dinner and dancing.

Action Steps

How will we gain or maintain the positive results from focusing on this right pole? What? Who? By when? Measures?

1. Review the budget.
2. Plan exceptions together.
3. Do the important things you both enjoy.

Greater Purpose Statement (GPS): Why balance this polarity?
MEMORABLE FLORIDA VACATION

Values = positive results from focusing on the left pole
- Flexible
- Freedom and independence
- Choices
- Energized
- Each day a new adventure

Values = positive results from focusing on the right pole
- Clarity
- Common understanding
- Security
- Reaching future goals
- Contingency plans

SPONTANEOUS and **PLANNED**

Early Warnings

Measurable indicators (things you can count) that will let you know that you are getting into the downside of this left pole.

1. Tense feeling.
2. Budget is overspent.
3. Missed important event.

- Ambiguous
- Vague
- Foolish risks
- Waste of time and money
- Potential for costly penalty

- Rigid
- Boundaries and restrictions
- Missed opportunities
- Bored
- Life is too monotonous

Early Warnings

Measurable indicators (things you can count) that will let you know that you are getting into the downside of this right pole.

1. Annie buys magazines.
2. Annie reads magazines to Matt.
3. "Watch the paint dry"

Fears = negative results from over focusing on the left pole *to the neglect* of the right pole

Fears = negative results from over focusing on the right pole *to the neglect* of the left pole

MISERABLE FLORIDA VACATION

Deeper Fear from lack of balance

Polarity Map #13

~

As a coach without Polarity Management, many questions could have been brought to bear on this situation, perhaps with a similar outcome. However, using a Polarity Map it is easy to define and appreciate the natural tendencies that attracted Matt and Annie to one another and to depict those natural tendencies in a way that will build their relationship and communication as a couple. Matt started our coaching session feeling helpless to solve a problem; with Polarity Management, Matt learned that what he was experiencing was not a problem to solve, but rather a polarity to manage. The Polarity Map brought Matt and Annie's natural tendencies into clear view and set the framework for a full coaching conversation—a conversation that will help Matt and Annie have a great two weeks!

~

Next we see two people struggle to work through difficult family dynamics as they use Polarity Coaching to lay the groundwork for meaningful interactions and reduce the risk of an unpredictable outcome.

Case Study #4
Directive and Participative

Carrie and I had been coaching for several months, and many of our coaching calls had been about her and her husband, their blended family, and the dreams and goals Carrie and her husband shared. This coaching session took a new turn beyond her immediate family to that of her husband and his father. Our Monday morning coaching call started with the usual inquiry.

"Good morning, Carrie; how was your week?" I inquired.

"It was okay," Carrie answered slowly.

"From the tone in your voice I'm sensing it wasn't really okay. Is there something about the week you'd like to coach on today?" I prompted.

Carrie paused momentarily, then answered, "Yes, actually there is. What happened this week has happened before, and it is causing a family problem."

Carrie paused again and then continued. "You see, my in-laws have a lake home. There is a lot of upkeep on the property, projects that my mother-in-law and father-in-law aren't able to tackle alone, so my husband Pete and his two brothers often help out. We went to help last weekend, and, unfortunately, it turned into a complete family disaster. Pete is pretty upset."

"That sounds serious," I acknowledged.

"Yes, it is serious," she agreed. "And I'd really like to get to the heart of this. There seems to be a recurring dilemma that isn't getting any better. When Pete, his brothers, and my father-in-law, John, work on a project together, it often ends up in an argument with the guys getting frustrated, dad getting mad, and the project going unfinished."

"What is an example?" I asked.

Carrie explained, "Pete's dad, John, called last week. He invited us to spend the weekend at the lake, and asked if Pete would help him tear down the deck and build a new one. Pete was not real excited about spending the whole weekend working on a deck, but agreed to do it under two conditions: first that his two brothers were there to help as well, and second that John would have the materials ready when they got there."

"Was that agreed to?" I questioned.

"Yes, everyone agreed to it. Pete's brothers said they'd be there and John agreed to have all the materials ready and waiting," Carrie answered.

"What went wrong?" I asked.

"We got there early Saturday morning, and Pete and his brothers started tearing out the old deck," Carried explained. "John did what he could to help, but before long he was tired and had to sit down to rest. This wasn't a problem, but then John began to direct the guys' work, pointing out the difference between what they were doing and how he'd like to see it done, basically giving orders. Pete and his brothers started getting frustrated. You see, the familiar pattern is that everyone starts on a project, John begins giving directions and doesn't listen to suggestions from anyone else, and the situation spirals down from there. Pete and his brothers get upset because they feel John isn't interested in their ideas. They feel they can't do anything right; they feel like they just can't please their dad."

"Pete's mom, Diane, and I were in the kitchen and we overheard the conversation starting down the all-too-familiar path. Together we just prayed they'd focus on the project and not get upset with one another," Carrie breathed an audible sigh.

"Carrie, it sounds like there is a family value here, a family value that is at risk. What is that value?" I inquired.

Carrie thought for a moment. "Family is important to us," she replied. "We want to have supportive and effective family relationships."

"Are supportive and effective family relationships important to Pete?" I asked.

"Oh, definitely!" Carrie confirmed.

Hoping to get a sense for the bigger picture, I asked, "What do you think about Pete's dad and his brothers? Are supportive and effective family relationships a value they share?"

Carrie considered the question. "Yes, I would say supportive family relationships are very important to John, Diane, and the whole family," she said. "They all want to spend time together, and they try to work effectively together as a way to show their support toward one another. It's just that once the buttons are pushed, all the good intentions fall apart."

Carrie was familiar with Polarity Management as we had created several Polarity Maps in the months of our coaching relationship. We coach by phone, and with both of us online, I prepare a map and e-mail it to Carrie for her to see while we discussed each point along the way.

"I'd like to start keying a Polarity Map, Carrie," I told her. "I think it will help us uncover the polarity underneath this tension, and the values and fears that are causing the relationship to spiral down in a negative way."

"Yes," Carrie agreed. "That has worked for us in the past; let's try it."
"Okay, let's get started," I said as I brought up a map template on my computer screen.

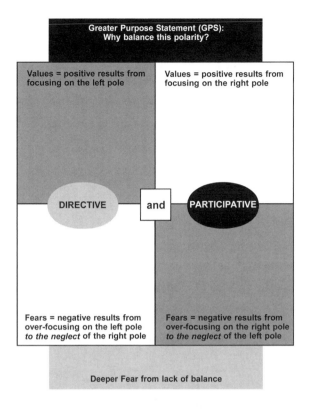

Polarity Map #1

From our conversation so far, it sounded as though supportive family relationships was the Greater Purpose and unsupportive family relationships would be the Deeper Fear. At this point,

Greater Purpose and Deeper Fear

I wasn't sure what the polarities were, so I asked another question.

"What do you think is at the heart of the matter, Carrie?"

"Wow—I'm not sure. I know they love each other," she said.

"Okay," I paused a moment and then continued, "They have love for each other; what don't they have?"

The problem started to became clear to Carrie.

"It may sound sort of childish, but it seems as though there is a feeling they have to prove something to one another. John wants recognition that he is still in charge, and the boys want their dad to

Name the Poles

acknowledge their work and their ability to get a job done. I think it boils down to respect. They want respect from one another, but they have a hard time giving respect to one another, so the day ends in confrontation. Would one of the poles be respect?" Carrie asked.

"Let's look a little deeper," I suggested. "Say more about respect."

Carrie continued, "As I mentioned, John is a very traditional person, and he sees himself as head of the family. John wants to make the decisions, give the direction, and because he is their father, he expects Pete and his brothers to follow his direction. He can be unreasonable about it. I think John forgets his sons are grown men and that they want to participate in the process beyond just doing the heavy lifting."

Now the Polarity Map was beginning to become clear. I typed in Directive and Participative as the two poles.

"What works in the current situation?" I asked, waiting to hear what values would surface.

"Well, John does give clear instructions, so things can be completed without a lot of questions. Everyone knows John is calling the shots, and if something goes wrong, John accepts the responsibility. I remember once they were working on the dock and several boards were cut the wrong length—John had no one to blame but himself, so he drove into town and bought more boards. And I would say that even though Pete and his brothers don't like being told what to do, John really does have a good eye for the big picture. In the short-term, it can be efficient."

Upper Left Quadrant for Directive

I keyed in the points Carrie made in the upside of the Directive pole.

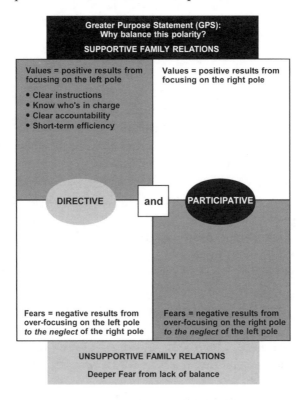

Polarity Map™ #2

"Okay, and what's not working in the current situation, Carrie?" I asked.

"Oh, that's easy. The story about the boards, well Pete knew they were being cut wrong and tried to tell his dad, but John is not so good at listening—he wouldn't listen to Pete's warning, and before Pete could say anything more, the boards were cut. Pete and his brothers have lots of good ideas, but their ideas aren't considered, and it's hard to get excited about doing a project when there is no real ownership of the project, no real buy-in. On a big project like this, they lack real interest in getting the job done, and they get distracted. Then when they get upset with John's way of handling things, they've been known to drop everything and literally go fishing."

> **Lower Left Quadrant for Directive**

"Carrie, I've been filling in the map as you've talked. I'm going to send it to you now."

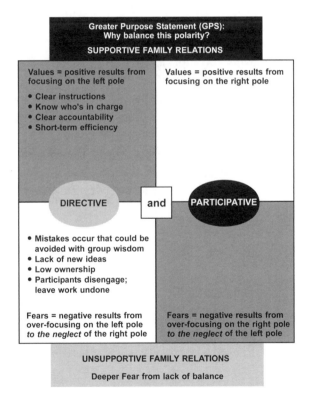

Polarity Map #3

Carrie received the e-mail within a few moments and we looked at the Polarity Map together.

"Yes!" Carrie remarked. "I think this is a Directive and Participative polarity. John will over focus on giving direction to the neglect of seeking participation, and the guys often find themselves in the downside of Directive, an argument starts, the guys give up, and John is left alone in the downside of the very pole he values. What John is trying to avoid is exactly what happens, and the work he wanted to get done is left undone. So the hope of a supportive family gathering is once again spiraling down to the Deeper Fear. It's only because they all really hold supportive family relationships as a mutual Greater Purpose that they keep trying, but they are definitely stuck in the downside of Directive right now."

"Okay, we're making progress," I affirmed

"Now let's take a look at the Participative pole. What about participation could be valuable?" I began.

"Well, I think my husband, Pete, would be happier! When he participates in a project like this, he wants to add positively to the job and work as a team. All the guys have good carpentry skills and good ideas. For example, Pete had some great ideas about changes to the railing and how to add a built-in bench, but John wasn't willing to consider his ideas. If John considered their ideas, I know the guys would have a greater sense of ownership to the project. I think there would also be more of a sense of family pride in incorporating everyone's ideas, commitment to seeing the job through to the end, and completing the project together."

Upper Right Quadrant for Participative

"Okay," I said in agreement, while keying in the points Carrie had highlighted. "That makes sense."

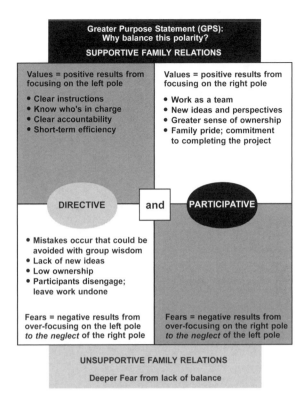

Polarity Map #4

"Now, if Pete and his brothers focused only on a participative style of getting things done, what would the downside of that look like?" I asked.

"Let me think," Carrie said trying to envision that scenario. "I know that when left to their own devices, there's a lack of direction and the guys spend a lot of time trying to outdo one another; I guess it's sibling rivalry or something.

> **Lower Right Quadrant for Participative**

Then if something goes wrong, no one seems to answer to the mistake. Without John directing, it takes them a lot longer to accomplish the work, and that takes away from the time they get to spend on the lake."

"Okay, Carrie, I've added the values and fears to the Participative pole and I'm e-mailing the updated map to you right now," I said as I attached the file and pressed send.

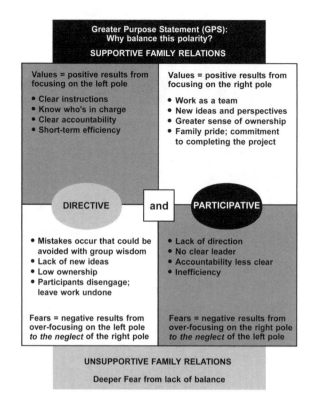

Polarity Map #5

Carrie opened the document and read what I had added. "Yes, this is it," she said and then hesitated. "No, wait. I also think there is a value of individual pride when they all participate in a positive way. Yes, there's a sense of family pride and individual pride."

"That sounds good. I'll make the change and resend," I responded making the change and resending.

Carrie opened the document again, and took another look. "Yes, this is it." This map reflects the tension, and last weekend we were definitely in the downside of Directive. It's clear that if we could tap into these values—into the upside of Directive and Participative—our family relationships would feel more supportive. The real key here is the greater purpose—family is of highest importance to them. The Polarity Map lays all this out and makes it understandable. I want Pete to see this Polarity Map! I think he will agree with the values and the fears."

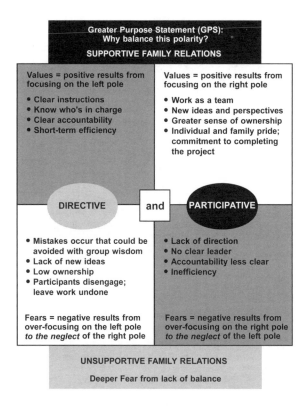

Polarity Map #6

"This map is incomplete without Action Steps and Early Warnings," I reminded her. "Keeping an eye on the Action Steps and Early Warnings will keep the family focused on the upside of Directive and Participative. Let me drop in that section of the Polarity Map and e-mail you a copy. I'll also drop in the Infinity Loop. The Infinity Loop simply shows

Infinity Loop

the energy force between the poles and how effective the men could be when paying attention to the values of both Directive and Participative. Clear Action Steps and Early Warnings will help make this happen."

"Sounds good!" Carrie answered. "When we meet next time, I'd like to meet in person, and I'd like to include Pete. I think it would help Pete to hear this and to walk through the map. I'll have to ask him, but I think he will be open to this. Then we could spend some time on the Action Steps and Early Warnings."

We made arrangements for our next coaching session to be held at their home. I e-mailed an updated Polarity Map to Carrie that included the Action Steps and Early Warnings sections, the Infinity Loop, and the Virtuous and Vicious Cycles.

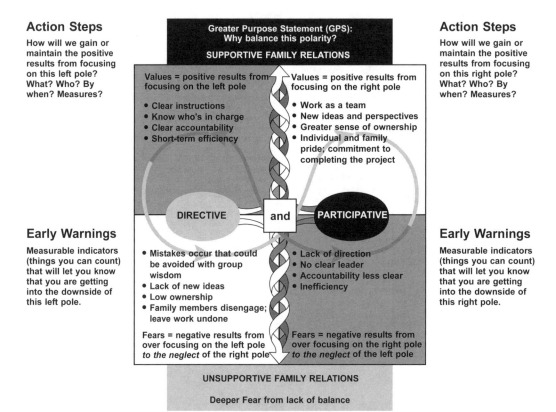

Action Steps

How will we gain or maintain the positive results from focusing on this left pole? What? Who? By when? Measures?

Action Steps

How will we gain or maintain the positive results from focusing on this right pole? What? Who? By when? Measures?

Greater Purpose Statement (GPS): Why balance this polarity?

SUPPORTIVE FAMILY RELATIONS

Values = positive results from focusing on the left pole

- Clear instructions
- Know who's in charge
- Clear accountability
- Short-term efficiency

Values = positive results from focusing on the right pole

- Work as a team
- New ideas and perspectives
- Greater sense of ownership
- Individual and family pride, commitment to completing the project

DIRECTIVE   and   PARTICIPATIVE

Early Warnings

Measurable indicators (things you can count) that will let you know that you are getting into the downside of this left pole.

- Mistakes occur that could be avoided with group wisdom
- Lack of new ideas
- Low ownership
- Family members disengage; leave work undone

Fears = negative results from over focusing on the left pole *to the neglect* of the right pole

- Lack of direction
- No clear leader
- Accountability less clear
- Inefficiency

Fears = negative results from over focusing on the right pole *to the neglect* of the left pole

Early Warnings

Measurable indicators (things you can count) that will let you know that you are getting into the downside of this right pole.

UNSUPPORTIVE FAMILY RELATIONS

Deeper Fear from lack of balance

Polarity Map #7

I transferred Carrie's Polarity Map to easel pad paper and arrived at their home the following week for our coaching session. Pete was there, and after our introductions, we got started.

With the map taped to the dining room wall, I began to walk Carrie and Pete through the map, starting in the upside of Directive as I had started with Carrie, and finishing with the concept of the Infinity Loop, and the Vicious and Virtuous Cycles.

Pete understood the concepts right away, and as we went through the upsides and downsides of Directive and Participative, he was able to see and understand where the tension was coming from. He was able to see why he would get frustrated, why he resented his dad's direction, and why nothing seemed to get done when John wasn't there. He confirmed that supportive family relationships was what kept him and his brothers trying to make it work and why they continued to commit to spending time at the lake together. Pete agreed that he felt stuck in the downside of Directive and had no clue how to get to the upside of Participative.

With that part of the map understood and agreed to, the next step was Action Steps and Early Warnings.

I began to explain, "Action Steps are meant to help you gain or maintain the positive results from focusing on a particular pole. They are meant to be specific, they can be measurable, they should be attainable and relevant to what your values are, and they can be time specific."

"Got it," answered Carrie. Pete nodded, with understanding.

"And Early Warnings let you know that you are getting into the downside of a particular pole," I continued. "As soon as you start experiencing an Early Warning, the idea is to focus on the Action Steps of the other pole. Early Warnings should also be measurable indicators so that you know it when you see it. For example, who will know you're in the downside, and how will they know it?"

Pete jumped in, "Let's start by looking at the Early Warnings of where we are now, the downside of Directive, and then the Action Steps we could take to move from where we are now, to the upside of Participative."

Carrie agreed.

I began by asking, "When there is a sense that there is too much focus on direction to the neglect of participation, what Early Warnings do you experience?"

Pete offered, "I can answer that. I get upset with Dad, and I find I need to walk away from the project and cool off."

"What triggers that feeling?" I asked.

"Mistakes are made that could have been avoided," Pete answered.

"Good, would an Early Warning be one mistake?" I offered.

> **Early Warnings due to an over focus on Directive**

"I would say one costly mistake," Pete answered.

"What else triggers that feeling?" I continued.

"The project isn't fun anymore; it becomes robotic since Dad is directing everyone's next move," Pete answered.

"Could we flip that to say 'Dad is not listening to suggestions?'" I asked.

"Sure," Pete agreed.

"Anything else?" I asked.

"The guys get frustrated," Carrie added. "I can hear when the guys start to grumble about John. It starts with a few strained words and goes from there."

"Would you say the frustration is being verbalized?" I offered.

"Yes, I would say that," Pete concurred.

I added this to the map and stepped away so that Carrie and Pete could read the Early Warnings.

Action Steps

How will we gain or maintain the positive results from focusing on this left pole? What? Who? By when? Measures?

Early Warnings

Measurable indicators (things you can count) that will let you know that you are getting into the downside of this left pole.

1. One costly mistake.
2. Dad isn't listening to suggestions.
3. Frustration is verbalized.

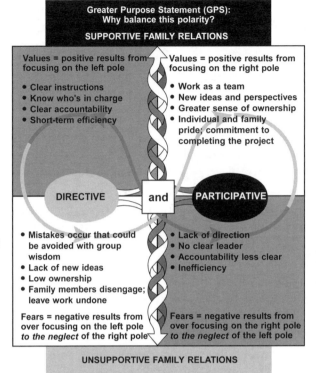

Greater Purpose Statement (GPS): Why balance this polarity?
SUPPORTIVE FAMILY RELATIONS

Values = positive results from focusing on the left pole

- Clear instructions
- Know who's in charge
- Clear accountability
- Short-term efficiency

Values = positive results from focusing on the right pole

- Work as a team
- New ideas and perspectives
- Greater sense of ownership
- Individual and family pride; commitment to completing the project

DIRECTIVE **and** PARTICIPATIVE

- Mistakes occur that could be avoided with group wisdom
- Lack of new ideas
- Low ownership
- Family members disengage; leave work undone

- Lack of direction
- No clear leader
- Accountability less clear
- Inefficiency

Fears = negative results from over focusing on the left pole *to the neglect* of the right pole

Fears = negative results from over focusing on the right pole *to the neglect* of the left pole

UNSUPPORTIVE FAMILY RELATIONS

Deeper Fear from lack of balance

Action Steps

How will we gain or maintain the positive results from focusing on this right pole? What? Who? By when? Measures?

Early Warnings

Measurable indicators (things you can count) that will let you know that you are getting into the downside of this right pole.

Polarity Map™ #8

"Following the Infinity Loop to the upside of Participative, what Action Steps are needed to gain or maintain the positive results from the Participative pole?" I asked.

> **Action Steps to refocus on Participative**

"In the case of the deck, I think we should all have participated in the design. My brothers and I have had a lot of carpentry experience, first as boys working with Dad, and more recently working on our own home projects. We all have good ideas to share," Pete said proudly. "And I'd like to be able to take a few breaks. Most of the time we start a project, and Dad just keeps going until it's finished. Before you know it, the weekend is over, and we haven't had any time to fish. This may sound funny, but Dad really pushes us; agreement on time to relax would be good for everyone, including Dad."

"What else?" I asked as I wrote those items on the easel paper.

> **Early Warnings due to an over focus on Participative**

"Last, I'd say I'd like Dad to listen. I'd like all of us to listen to one another and be supportive of one another, especially when something looks wrong to one of us. We should be able to pause, gather together, look at the situation, and then proceed when we've all agreed what direction to take," Pete added firmly.

We all took another look at the map.

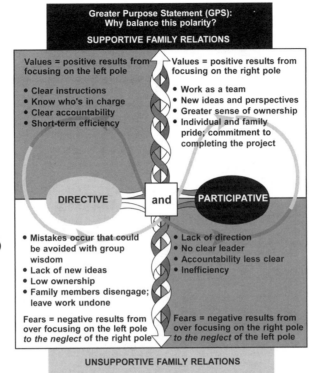

Action Steps

How will we gain or maintain the positive results from focusing on this left pole? What? Who? By when? Measures?

Early Warnings

Measurable indicators (things you can count) that will let you know that you are getting into the downside of this left pole.

1. One costly mistake.
2. Dad isn't listening to suggestions.
3. Frustration is verbalized.

Greater Purpose Statement (GPS): Why balance this polarity?
SUPPORTIVE FAMILY RELATIONS

Values = positive results from focusing on the left pole

- Clear instructions
- Know who's in charge
- Clear accountability
- Short-term efficiency

Values = positive results from focusing on the right pole

- Work as a team
- New ideas and perspectives
- Greater sense of ownership
- Individual and family pride; commitment to completing the project

DIRECTIVE and **PARTICIPATIVE**

- Mistakes occur that could be avoided with group wisdom
- Lack of new ideas
- Low ownership
- Family members disengage; leave work undone

Fears = negative results from over focusing on the left pole *to the neglect* of the right pole

- Lack of direction
- No clear leader
- Accountability less clear
- Inefficiency

Fears = negative results from over focusing on the right pole *to the neglect* of the left pole

UNSUPPORTIVE FAMILY RELATIONS

Deeper Fear from lack of balance

Action Steps

How will we gain or maintain the positive results from focusing on this right pole? What? Who? By when? Measures?

1. All participate in design.
2. Agree on time to relax.
3. Listen to one another's suggestions and concerns.
4. Forge agreement on how to proceed.

Early Warnings

Measurable indicators (things you can count) that will let you know that you are getting into the downside of this right pole.

Polarity Map #9

"Okay. Now, how will you know when you are over focused on participation to the neglect of John's direction?" I asked.

Pete replied, "We start wasting time. When Dad isn't there, we start talking and stop working. We might decide to blow off the entire weekend. Or sometimes we spend too much time trying to present the merits of our own way of doing things, and it takes a long time to come to consensus and get anything done."

"Okay, what else?" I asked.

"When we're focused on ourselves and leave Dad out of the conversation, he feels rejected. I think he has a high need to be the leader of the family in any situation, and he will try to step back into control. When he does this, it comes out in anger," Pete said slowly, showing the sadness that accompanied his words.

"How does this make you feel?" I asked.

"I know we have unresolved issues," Pete answered. "When that happens, our traditional family values and deep desire to support one another (Greater Purpose Statement) usually takes over, and we generally let Dad take over."

I finished writing in the Early Warnings for Participative, and stepped aside for Carrie and Pete to see the map.

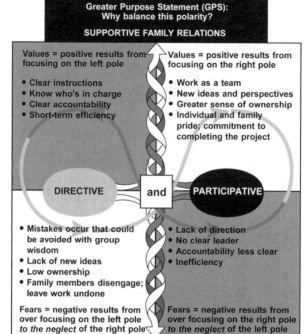

Action Steps

How will we gain or maintain the positive results from focusing on this left pole? What? Who? By when? Measures?

Action Steps

How will we gain or maintain the positive results from focusing on this right pole? What? Who? By when? Measures?

1. All participate in design.
2. Agree on time to relax.
3. Listen to one another's suggestions and concerns.
4. Forge agreement on how to proceed.

Greater Purpose Statement (GPS):
Why balance this polarity?
SUPPORTIVE FAMILY RELATIONS

Values = positive results from focusing on the left pole

- Clear instructions
- Know who's in charge
- Clear accountability
- Short-term efficiency

Values = positive results from focusing on the right pole

- Work as a team
- New ideas and perspectives
- Greater sense of ownership
- Individual and family pride; commitment to completing the project

DIRECTIVE **and** PARTICIPATIVE

Early Warnings

Measurable indicators (things you can count) that will let you know that you are getting into the downside of this left pole.

1. One costly mistake.
2. Dad isn't listening to suggestions.
3. Frustration is verbalized.

- Mistakes occur that could be avoided with group wisdom
- Lack of new ideas
- Low ownership
- Family members disengage; leave work undone

Fears = negative results from over focusing on the left pole *to the neglect of the right pole*

- Lack of direction
- No clear leader
- Accountability less clear
- Inefficiency

Fears = negative results from over focusing on the right pole *to the neglect of the left pole*

Early Warnings

Measurable indicators (things you can count) that will let you know that you are getting into the downside of this right pole.

1. Time is wasted.
2. Difficulty forming consensus.
3. Dad is left out.
4. Dad is angry.

UNSUPPORTIVE FAMILY RELATIONS

Deeper Fear from lack of balance

Polarity Map #10

"So if you were in the downside of Participative, what steps would you take to gain or maintain the positive results from John's direction?" I asked.

"First, I think we need to lighten up, me included. Second, I would say we have to give Dad final say. After all, he buys the materials and Dad and Mom have to live with the outcome—it is their home. If we know he considers our ideas, I don't think any of us would have a problem with him making a final decision, especially if that was agreed to up front," Pete said supportively. "At the same time, I'd like to see Dad give us the credit we deserve for the time we spend and for a

> **Action Steps to refocus on Directive**

> **Virtuous and Vicious Cycles**

job well done, and we need to enjoy the work and the time together—that's important," Pete affirmed.

Finishing the map, I stepped away so that we could all take a look.

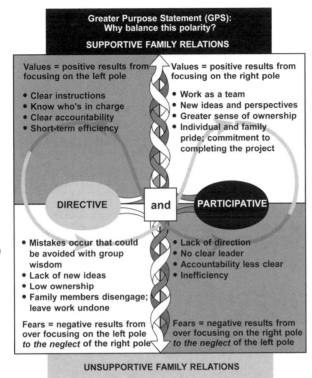

Action Steps

How will we gain or maintain the positive results from focusing on this left pole? What? Who? By when? Measures?

1. Everyone lighten up.
2. Dad is final decision maker.
3. Dad gives credit where credit is due.
4. Enjoy the work and time together.

Early Warnings

Measurable indicators (things you can count) that will let you know that you are getting into the downside of this left pole.

1. One costly mistake.
2. Dad isn't listening to suggestions.
3. Frustration is verbalized.

Greater Purpose Statement (GPS): Why balance this polarity?
SUPPORTIVE FAMILY RELATIONS

Values = positive results from focusing on the left pole

- Clear instructions
- Know who's in charge
- Clear accountability
- Short-term efficiency

Values = positive results from focusing on the right pole

- Work as a team
- New ideas and perspectives
- Greater sense of ownership
- Individual and family pride; commitment to completing the project

DIRECTIVE and **PARTICIPATIVE**

- Mistakes occur that could be avoided with group wisdom
- Lack of new ideas
- Low ownership
- Family members disengage; leave work undone

- Lack of direction
- No clear leader
- Accountability less clear
- Inefficiency

Fears = negative results from over focusing on the left pole *to the neglect* of the right pole

Fears = negative results from over focusing on the right pole *to the neglect* of the left pole

UNSUPPORTIVE FAMILY RELATIONS

Deeper Fear from lack of balance

Action Steps

How will we gain or maintain the positive results from focusing on this right pole? What? Who? By when? Measures?

1. All participate in design.
2. Agree on time to relax.
3. Listen to one another's suggestions and concerns.
4. Forge agreement on how to proceed.

Early Warnings

Measurable indicators (things you can count) that will let you know that you are getting into the downside of this right pole.

1. Time is wasted.
2. Difficulty forming consensus.
3. Dad is left out.
4. Dad is angry.

Polarity Map #11

"This map tells the whole story, and it's so easy to see where we get sidetracked and cycle down this downward arrow," Pete said drawing our attention to the downward spiraling arrow.

"It does tell the whole story, and we can see how to stay on track toward the family's Greater Purpose," Carrie said pointing to the upward spiraling arrow.

"Yes," I said to reinforce, "it is easy to see how the negative results of Directive and Participative can create a Vicious Cycle toward your Deeper Fear, and by paying attention to Action Steps and Early Warnings, the family can experience the positive aspects of Directive and Participative and move in a Virtuous Cycle toward your supportive family relations."

Carrie and Pete were delighted with the map, but there was more to do.

"Carrie and Pete, what can you do with this Polarity Map, and your new insight?" I asked.

Pete jumped in to answer, "I want to use the map to build and maintain common ground in the family, and I think Dad and my brothers will be able to see this. We are a close family, and we want to be supportive of one another. I know this will help!"

I added the words "building and maintaining common ground" to the top margin of the Polarity Map.

Name the Map

Building and Maintaining Common Ground

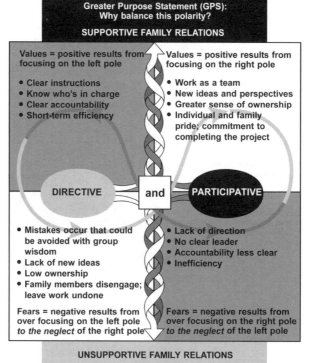

Action Steps

How will we gain or maintain the positive results from focusing on this left pole? What? Who? By when? Measures?

1. Everyone lighten up.
2. Dad is final decision maker.
3. Dad gives credit where credit is due.
4. Enjoy the work and time together.

Early Warnings

Measurable indicators (things you can count) that will let you know that you are getting into the downside of this left pole.

1. One costly mistake.
2. Dad isn't listening to suggestions.
3. Frustration is verbalized.

Action Steps

How will we gain or maintain the positive results from focusing on this right pole? What? Who? By when? Measures?

1. All participate in design.
2. Agree on time to relax.
3. Listen to one another's suggestions and concerns.
4. Forge agreement on how to proceed.

Early Warnings

Measurable indicators (things you can count) that will let you know that you are getting into the downside of this right pole.

1. Time is wasted.
2. Difficulty forming consensus.
3. Dad is left out.
4. Dad is angry.

Greater Purpose Statement (GPS): Why balance this polarity?
SUPPORTIVE FAMILY RELATIONS

Values = positive results from focusing on the left pole
- Clear instructions
- Know who's in charge
- Clear accountability
- Short-term efficiency

Values = positive results from focusing on the right pole
- Work as a team
- New ideas and perspectives
- Greater sense of ownership
- Individual and family pride; commitment to completing the project

DIRECTIVE **and** PARTICIPATIVE

- Mistakes occur that could be avoided with group wisdom
- Lack of new ideas
- Low ownership
- Family members disengage; leave work undone

- Lack of direction
- No clear leader
- Accountability less clear
- Inefficiency

Fears = negative results from over focusing on the left pole *to the neglect of the right pole*

Fears = negative results from over focusing on the right pole *to the neglect of the left pole*

UNSUPPORTIVE FAMILY RELATIONS

Deeper Fear from lack of balance

Polarity Map #12

Carrie added, "John will be able to see that he is respected for his leadership because it's clear there is value in his direction. This Polarity Map can help John, Pete, and his brothers all see that there is a downside to ignoring Participative, that if left unchecked it will begin a downward spiral to unsupportive family relations."

"Yes, that's true, and by focusing on the Action Steps and Early Warnings, it's clear to see how to gain and maintain the positive results of each pole," Pete echoed.

"How do you feel about this situation right now?" I asked.

"I feel hopeful," Carrie answered.

"What can you do in the next week before our next coaching session?" I asked.

"We are going to the cabin again this weekend to finish the deck," Pete clarified. "I'm going to start the weekend with a family meeting and talk about supportive family relations and how direction and participation has had both positive and negative effects on our family relationships. My hope is that they will understand this and together we can watch for the Early Warnings and remember the Action Steps that we need to take. I'll give it a try and see what happens."

We said our good-byes.

The next week, our Monday morning coaching call started with the usual inquiry.

"Good morning, Carrie, how was your week?" I inquired.

"It was really good!" Carrie answered quickly.

"From the tone in your voice, I'm sensing you are excited about something," I prompted.

"Yes, I am," Carrie replied. "We had a great weekend at the lake!"

~

With Polarity Coaching, Pete could see the family situation as a whole, rather than simply the parts, and he is better equipped to influence the conversations and potential outcomes of future family gatherings. Pete now understands the common bond that holds the family together and with that knowledge, he can watch for opportunities to positively engage family members.

~

In the next case we find Wendy, a client who is unable to see the value of the interdependent pair in her polarity. Wendy is convinced that her plan and her preferred value is the only way to achieve her greater purpose. She resists the nonpreferred pole of the interdependent pair because she can see no value there—all she can see is the downside of nonpreferred pole. This case demonstrates the principle that if you over focus on one pole to the neglect of the other and become stuck, first you get the downside of the pole on which you over focus and then you get the downside of the nonpreferred pole as well; you get what you are most working to avoid. Watch as the coach skillfully holds the client while coaching through the resistance, names the interdependent pole, and moves the client forward to a balanced outcome.

Case Study #5
Activity and Rest

Wendy's story is about a solution that became a problem. This year, Wendy's annual physical came with a few surprises. Her doctor pointed out that over a period of three years, she had gained nearly 20 pounds. The weight gain wasn't a surprise; however, her blood pressure reading and the results of her cholesterol test had fallen outside normal ranges and that was a big surprise. Her doctor recommended she begin to exercise on a regular basis and make changes to her diet. After discussing this at length with her doctor, she was determined to make changes and do whatever it took to lose the extra weight and improve her overall health.

Wendy started by making some thoughtful changes to her diet, and then she joined a fitness club and hired a personal trainer. Getting to the club and doing her 90-minute workout had soon become her number one priority; she went faithfully five times a week. Although other important areas of her life were getting less of her attention, she continued to be committed to her new life style. With the diet changes and the exercise, the weight started to come off, and her overall energy level began to increase. She found she was able to get up earlier and get more done around the house before starting her busy day of single parenting her two pre-teens and working hard to manage a demanding job. Wendy had been struggling a bit, but generally doing well to keep on top of her responsibilities while focusing on her diet and increasing her exercise regimen—she was keeping it all in high gear and seeing results.

After about four months, however, things began to change. She began to feel overwhelmed by the constant focus on the diet and exercise regimen, and felt the push back from her kids, as they weren't getting the time and attention they had gotten in the past. She realized their homework wasn't being attended to as it should be and that laundry piles were bigger than she would like. She tried to pack the kids' homework and activities into less time, but noticed that the time spent together was more stressful than before. Although she felt her new life style had positive benefits, she was also experiencing a downside of continual focus on activity that was getting harder and harder to ignore.

Coming home one Friday night at the end of a very long week, she could not bring herself to prepare a nice meal, so she ordered pizza. After enjoying the pizza with her family, she collapsed into bed. The next morning, Wendy didn't get up and go to the club as was now her normal routine; she slept in and later that day took the kids to a movie, where they all relished their traditional movie popcorn and soda. They had a great time together, but later she felt guilty about eating the popcorn and blowing off her workout.

Deep down she felt she hadn't been spending enough time with her kids or with the other important people in her life, and that weekend was the start in a decline of her weekly workouts. Wendy began to realize that her job, spending quality time with the kids, maintaining the house, and going to the club five times a week had gotten to be too much. Within two months, she had stopped going to the club altogether.

Despite less exercise, Wendy initially maintained her lower weight by eating less, but then her energy level dropped. She found herself feeling tired during the day and fell back into the all-too-familiar habit of munching on a candy bar at noon to get a temporary energy bounce. She was on her way back into a pattern that would not produce the results she wanted.

Weeks passed, and Wendy's weight started creeping back on. She was disappointed in herself and began to feel depressed and tired even though she was getting enough sleep. She knew she was slipping back to her previous habits and was disappointed in her inability to maintain her exercise routine and her goal weight. She had fallen back into the downside of rest. That's when Wendy called a coach.

We met for our first coaching session. Having established our coaching relationship, Wendy started by telling me that her goal was to get back to the club and that she had hired me to get her back on track and to hold her accountable.

"As your coach, I will support, encourage, and hold you accountable to meet your goal," I told her. "To get started, I'd like to ask you a few questions. First, tell me, Wendy, what is it that you are hoping for?"

Wendy responded quickly. "When I was going to the club five times a week, I felt toned and energized, and I had lost some of the weight I needed to lose—doctor's orders," she added. "Then I slipped back into old, unhealthy habits. Now I want to get back on track and get back to the club."

"I'm curious, Wendy. What do you think got you off track? What happened that caused you to slip back into old habits?"

Wendy's reply was straightforward. "I lost my focus. It seemed as though work was getting in the way and I felt a push back from my kids. I was behind in the routine chores at home and my friends couldn't understand why I wasn't returning their calls. I gave in to the pressure I was feeling, fell out of my routine, and then couldn't seem to get myself back into it." Reflecting back, Wendy continued, "It all started one Friday night. I came home after a long and difficult workweek, and I remember feeling like I really needed a break from my structured routine. I just didn't feel like cooking a nice meal, so I ordered delivery. I ate the pizza with the kids and then collapsed into bed. The alarm went off the next morning, and I should have gotten up and gone to the club, but instead I turned off the alarm and went back to sleep. I was just too tired to get up and go."

"You must have needed a break," I responded.

"Yes, I guess I did. I have a very fast pace that I have to keep in order to manage my work, the kids, and getting to the club five times a week, not to mention the laundry, the errands—it was getting to be too much and I felt I just couldn't do it anymore. I was feeling burned out," Wendy said nodding.

I continue, "So it sounds like while you were focused on your exercise activities, you were burning out trying to keep up the pace."

"Yes, I guess you could say that." Pausing and thinking, Wendy said slowly, "I was focused on a strict routine for so long, and like you said, I needed a break—it's hard to believe that what I wanted caused a problem for me."

"What is your intuition telling you right now, Wendy?"

Wendy thought for a moment and then said with a disappointed tone, "I'm almost back to where I started. I have a hard time keeping up a program and making it an ongoing lifestyle change. But I also know I really want to maintain a healthy lifestyle, and I have to keep my weight down." Wendy continued with renewed determination, "Maintaining a healthy lifestyle is very important to me, so I have to do it."

Name the Map

"So maintaining a healthy lifestyle is very important to you," I asked to confirm.

"Yes, it is," Wendy confirmed.

"But you feel stuck?" I asked somewhat rhetorically.

"Yes, I feel stuck," Wendy confirmed again.

"Paint me a picture of that healthy lifestyle, Wendy—what are you doing and how are you feeling?" I wondered aloud.

Upper Left Quadrant for Activity

As Wendy described her picture of a healthy lifestyle, she was focused and clear: she wanted to feel strong and energetic; she wanted to feel toned and to be at least 10 pounds lighter as her doctor had advised. Yet I knew she was not getting what she wanted, and the normal flow from her activity to a place of rest was not happening. I began drawing a Polarity Map.

I wrote "Healthy Lifestyle" in the Greater Purpose box at the top of the map, and "Unhealthy Lifestyle" as the Deeper Fear in the bottom box.

Greater Purpose and Deeper Fear

Thinking from a polarity perspective, I knew one of the poles was Activity so I added that and included the values Wendy had described of feeling strong, energetic, toned muscles, and maintaining a healthy weight.

Name a Pole

Maintaining a Healthy Lifestyle

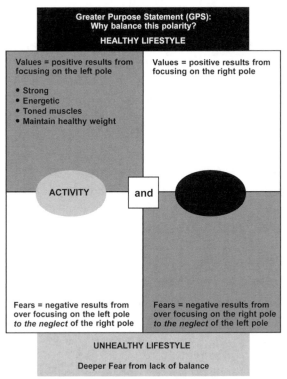

Greater Purpose Statement (GPS):
Why balance this polarity?
HEALTHY LIFESTYLE

Values = positive results from
focusing on the left pole

- Strong
- Energetic
- Toned muscles
- Maintain healthy weight

Values = positive results from
focusing on the right pole

ACTIVITY **and**

Fears = negative results from
over focusing on the left pole
to the neglect of the right pole

Fears = negative results from
over focusing on the right pole
to the neglect of the left pole

UNHEALTHY LIFESTYLE

Deeper Fear from lack of balance

Polarity Map #1

I affirmed Wendy's vision and asked, "Tell me again, Wendy, where did you get stuck before and what did you learn from that experience that might help you now?"

Wendy again recalled her feeling of burn out from her strict 90-minute workout routine and said that she had needed a break. She had been feeling tension, she felt a pull from family and friends, and she admitted that she probably hadn't been getting enough rest for the four months she had been focused on her commitment to work out five times each week. "There just weren't enough hours in each day, and it was challenging trying to get everything done!" Wendy admitted.

I listened carefully as she spoke and added the words "need a break," "burned out," "tension," and "challenging" to the map as the downside of Activity.

> **Lower Left Quadrant**
> **for Activity**

I also added Rest as the interdependent pole of Activity, as it sounded like the tension was between activity, and rest and relaxation.

> **Name a Pole**

80

Maintaining a Healthy Lifestyle

Greater Purpose Statement (GPS): Why balance this polarity? **HEALTHY LIFESTYLE**	
Values = positive results from focusing on the left pole • Strong • Energetic • Toned muscles • Maintain healthy weight	Values = positive results from focusing on the right pole
ACTIVITY — and — **REST**	
• Need a break • Burned out • Tension • Challenging	
Fears = negative results from over focusing on the left pole *to the neglect* of the right pole	Fears = negative results from over focusing on the right pole *to the neglect* of the left pole
UNHEALTHY LIFESTYLE Deeper Fear from lack of balance	

Polarity Map #2

"I'm curious, Wendy", I started, "can you describe how you feel when you are able to relax, and when you have had enough rest?"

Wendy spoke strongly, "This isn't about rest! This is about developing a plan to get back to the gym and to stay there! I feel like I'm stuck in this negative space," Wendy answered. "I'm beginning to feel dull and weak, and of course I have lost muscle tone. Without exercise, I have gained back some of the weight I lost. I'm just not at my best, and I feel like I'm in a Vicious Cycle—do you know what I mean?"

"Yes, I do know what you mean," I said sincerely as I wrote in Wendy's descriptors for the downside of the Rest pole.

Lower Right Quadrant for Rest

What I heard was Wendy's description of the downside of Rest, though she got there by over-focusing on activity. She was not getting what she wanted and the normal flow from the downside of Activity to the upside of Rest was blocked.

Maintaining a Healthy Lifestyle

Greater Purpose Statement (GPS):
Why balance this polarity?
HEALTHY LIFESTYLE

Values = positive results from focusing on the left pole

- Strong
- Energetic
- Toned muscles
- Maintain healthy weight

Values = positive results from focusing on the right pole

ACTIVITY

REST

- Need a break
- Burned out
- Tension
- Challenging

Fears = negative results from over focusing on the left pole *to the neglect* of the right pole

Fears = negative results from over focusing on the right pole *to the neglect* of the left pole

UNHEALTHY LIFESTYLE

Deeper Fear from lack of balance

Polarity Map #3

Wendy was stuck and unable to see the interdependent nature of Activity and Rest and how rest could be part of her plan. Following the natural flow of the polarity, Wendy had moved from the upside of Activity to the downside of Activity, and then unable to move to the upside of Rest or back to the upside of Activity, she found herself in the downside of Rest as over time a continued over focus on one pole will lead to the downside of both. She had experienced the downside of both poles and was now stuck in the downside of the pole she had been hoping to avoid. I understood clearly that Wendy's goal was the upside of Activity; however, stuck where she was, she was not able to move toward her goal. I knew that she wanted to hold tightly to Activity, her preferred pole, and as much as coaching will work for Wendy, there is a process. At some point, she would be forced to focus on Rest or continue to spiral down to her Deeper Fear. When in the downside of both poles, it was my job to help Wendy see and understand how she got there.

When a client seems to hold tightly to a single pole, the normal flow from that pole to its interdependent pair seems blocked. Recognizing this and knowing how polarities work, I needed to coach her through the resistance model, also known as the Getting Unstuck™ Model[1] in order for her to supplement the "either/or" mindset and see and appreciate "both" Activity "and" Rest. I knew that unless Wendy could see the need to balance activity and rest as an inter-dependent pair of a polarity to manage, she would continue to be blocked and eventually she would spiral toward her Deeper Fear, an unhealthy lifestyle.

Wendy went on, "Just a few months ago, I was feeling stronger and my weight was better. I want to get back to taking care of myself again. I want to get back to the gym and back to my healthy lifestyle!"

Wendy most valued the positive aspects of Activity and held to her belief that Activity was the single solution toward a healthy lifestyle. Activity was indeed a solution toward a healthy lifestyle; however, this was only half of the solution—a one-sided view.

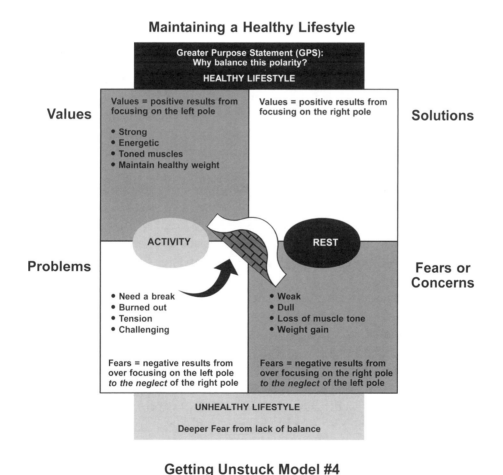

Getting Unstuck Model #4

---

[1] *Polarity Management: Identifying and Managing Unsolvable Problems*, Barry Johnson, Ph.D. HRD Press, Inc., Amherst: MA

There are five steps in the Getting Unstuck Model. Step 1 is to recognize the value of the preferred pole. In Step 2, the coach names the other pole and seeks to understand and affirm the legitimate fears and concerns of the downside of the other pole and then points to the interdependent nature of poles. This helps the client begin to see them as an interdependent pair to manage—to see that they need both poles. In Step 3, the coach asks if there is a way to pursue the upside of the other pole while (Step 4) holding on to the upside of the preferred pole in order to attain the Greater Purpose (Step 5).

"Okay, let me try to summarize what I've heard so far," I began. "I can see that a healthy lifestyle and getting back to the gym for regular workouts is what you are focused on. You value the way you physically felt and looked, and you are absolutely right about activity being essential to a healthy lifestyle. It also sounds like there was a problem. Without a needed break, without rest, the strenuous routine became too much, and you weren't able to maintain the routine."

"Yes, that's right!" Wendy confirmed.

I continued, "I also hear your concerns about losing muscle tone, regaining the weight, and the strong desire to move back toward that physical fitness that you value, yet you don't seem able to do it. And you spoke earlier of the vicious cycle you felt you were in and that you wanted to get back to focus on a healthy lifestyle."

"Right," Wendy confirmed again.

"I'm curious, Wendy, as you envision yourself beginning again with your exercise program, what will increase your chance of success?" I asked.

At first, Wendy was silent, then she answered, "I'm counting on you, Coach." Wendy answered gaining confidence as she spoke.

"Yes, and as your coach, it is my job to ask questions that help stretch you in various ways and work through any blind spots you may have," I answered.

"Do you think I have a blind spot?" Wendy asked in a surprised tone.

"Everyone has blind spots, Wendy," I assured her.

"Let me ask you this," I began again, "what other aspects of a healthy life-style come to mind in addition to a solid workout routine?"

Wendy thought for a long moment and then answered, "I would say a healthy lifestyle includes spending time with those you love and time with family and friends, and I long for some quiet time for myself to relax or read."

Upper Right Quadrant for Rest

"Okay, so in addition to the activity of a solid workout routine, there is also a place for family and friends and time for rest and relaxation?" I asked to confirm.

"Sure, everyone needs that at some point," Wendy answered carefully. "When I get the rest I need, I feel like facing the day, you know, rejuvenated and relaxed. I feel better about my work and I'm happy in my relationships with others. The tension decreases and I'm more at ease."

"Wendy, are you able to hold both the activity of a workout routine and the time you need to rest, to feel rejuvenated and relaxed, as two parts of a healthy lifestyle?" I inquired as I wrote "rejuvenated," "relaxed," "happy," and "at ease" on the upside of the Rest pole.

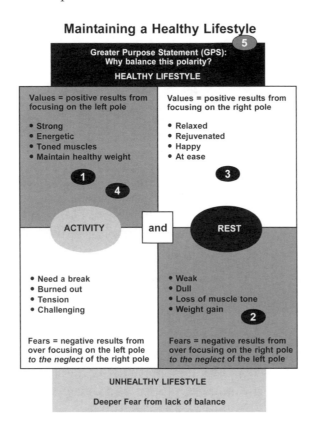

Polarity Map #5

"I think I can. Yes, I think I can see that now. Both are important to the healthy lifestyle we have been talking about—the healthy lifestyle that I want to maintain," she replied with a knowing smile.

I drew in an Infinity Loop and the Vicious and Virtuous Cycle spiraling arrows and then turned the Polarity Map I had been drawing toward Wendy. "Both are important to a healthy lifestyle," I echoed. Wendy was now looking at the map.

Maintaining a Healthy Lifestyle

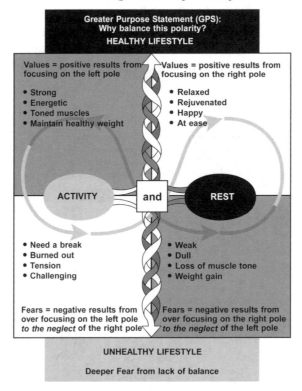

Polarity Map #6

I explained that what she was looking at was a Polarity Map and that a Polarity Map can be used to demonstrate what is missing in a given situation, how to get "unstuck," and what is needed to achieve balance and her greater purpose.

Wendy looked intently at the map.

I drew Wendy's attention first to the box on the top of the map and clarified that a healthy lifestyle was her Greater Purpose, and then to the box on the bottom of the map noting an unhealthy lifestyle as her Deeper Fear. I explained that the part of living a healthy lifestyle that she wanted coaching on was getting more activity.

Pointing at the upper left quadrant of the Polarity Map, I continued to check in with what I had heard: "Wendy, I heard you say that you feel that a healthy lifestyle means getting to the club five times a week for your workout, and when you have accomplished this, you feel strong and energetic, your muscles are toned, and you can maintain a healthy weight."

Wendy looked at the map. "Yes, that's right," she agreed.

I continued. "Yet, what you needed was a break from the demanding routine and you felt burned out—very different than what you are striving for," I said as I pointed at the lower left quadrant under the word Activity.

"Yes, that's right," Wendy responded carefully.

With the Polarity Map between us on the table, I shifted our attention to the right side of the map. I explained that when we were able to confirm the negative picture of too much rest, she might find it helpful to explore the aspects of rest that are valuable.

I explained that while she was focused on Activity, she had neglected the upside of the other pole. Wendy had not made time for the adequate rest she needed, and therefore, she was unable to experience the upside of Rest, which she had described as a relaxed and rejuvenated feeling and being better able to manage other aspects of her life. She had been able to see the negative aspects of Rest, but she was blind to the positive aspects of Rest that she needed.

"Okay," Wendy added. "I think I understand. Although I was experiencing the negative aspects of Activity and Rest I still couldn't see the positive aspects of Rest."

"That's right," I confirmed. "There was a shift from the downside of Activity to the downside of rest and ultimately you felt weak and dull, and you would not be able to maintain the healthy weight that you want to maintain. This, combined with a fear of returning to the downside of Activity, is what caused you to get stuck in the downside of Rest. As you can see, an over focus on Rest to the neglect of Activity isn't going to get you to your Greater Purpose either. In fact, it will set a Vicious Cycle into motion."

"A Vicious Cycle?" Wendy questioned. "Yes, I felt I was in a Vicious Cycle." Wendy paused to think all this through.

"A component of the Polarity Map is the Vicious Cycle," I explained, "A downward spiraling arrow that depicts that the bottom quadrants of the map lead to an Unhealthy Lifestyle. Likewise, when you experience the top quadrants of the map, you experience what's called the Virtuous Cycle, and this moves you to your goal—a Healthy Lifestyle." I added as I pointed to the Virtuous Cycle upward spiraling arrow.

> **Vicious and Virtuous Cycle**

Wendy understood this concept right away. Now she began asking the questions: "All of this means I need to find a balance between Activity and Rest?"

"Exactly!" I said.

I reaffirmed her instincts and we reviewed the Infinity Loop. Wendy could see that once she had experienced an over focus on Activity to the neglect of Rest, she was blind to the upside of Rest, which led her instead to the downside of Rest. Now, experiencing the downside of Rest she was naturally trying to begin her way back up the Infinity Loop in pursuit of the upside of Activity.

> **Infinity Loop**

"In this case, Wendy," I continued, "Activity and Rest are an interdependent pair that both need attention in order to achieve the healthy lifestyle that you desire. Paying attention to both and maintaining the balance between the inter-dependent pair initiate the Virtuous Cycle toward the healthy lifestyle you want to maintain," I continued.

Wendy looked at the map again. "How will I know when I'm over focused on Activity to the neglect of Rest? I mean, I can see from the map that I will feel strong and energetic when I am focusing on activity, my muscles will be toned, and I'll be managing my weight. All this is true and I love that, but how will I know when I start to over focus? I want to know when I need a break. I don't want to get down and feel exhausted and burned out again; I want to avoid the tension I was feeling before," Wendy clarified.

That was the perfect lead-in for introducing Action Steps and Early Warnings.

I explained to Wendy that Action Steps are used as a way to gain or maintain her Greater Purpose. Action Steps should be measurable and provide a basis for accountability and self-correction. Action Steps answer the questions such as "What do I need to do, and by when?" They are the steps to keep one focused on both poles as well as when to shift poles to maintain balance.

I explained that Early Warnings are indicators that allow us to anticipate and respond to the downside experiences. Acknowledging a downside quickly and responding with Action Steps keep the Infinity Loop in the upside of the two poles. I drew in the space for Action Steps and Early Warnings and turned the Polarity Map so that Wendy could study it.

Maintaining a Healthy Lifestyle

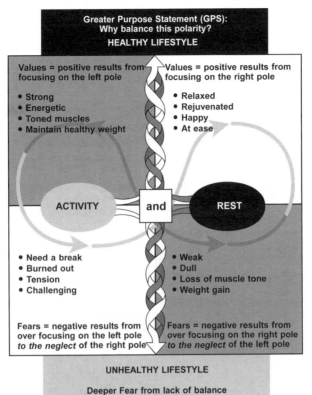

Action Steps

How will we gain or maintain the positive results from focusing on this left pole? What? Who? By when? Measures?

Early Warnings

Measurable indicators (things you can count) that will let you know that you are getting into the downside of this left pole.

Action Steps

How will we gain or maintain the positive results from focusing on this right pole? What? Who? By when? Measures?

Early Warnings

Measurable indicators (things you can count) that will let you know that you are getting into the downside of this right pole.

Within the map:

Greater Purpose Statement (GPS): Why balance this polarity? **HEALTHY LIFESTYLE**

Values = positive results from focusing on the left pole
- Strong
- Energetic
- Toned muscles
- Maintain healthy weight

Values = positive results from focusing on the right pole
- Relaxed
- Rejuvenated
- Happy
- At ease

ACTIVITY and **REST**

- Need a break
- Burned out
- Tension
- Challenging

- Weak
- Dull
- Loss of muscle tone
- Weight gain

Fears = negative results from over focusing on the left pole *to the neglect* of the right pole

Fears = negative results from over focusing on the right pole *to the neglect* of the left pole

UNHEALTHY LIFESTYLE

Deeper Fear from lack of balance

Polarity Map #7

"I'm still a little unsure of how Action Steps and Early Warnings would work," Wendy said thoughtfully.

Hoping to discover what her Early Warnings had been, I asked Wendy what negative experiences she had had that led to that Friday night of pizza.

Wendy admitted she had felt barely able to manage for quite some time, and with the job and the kids requiring every spare moment, she was feeling a lot of pressure and stress.

"What else do you know about what you were experiencing? What else was happening physically? How were your family and friends reacting?" I asked.

She explained that her first sign starts in her neck. "I carry my stress in the back of my neck," she

> **Early Warnings due to an over focus on Activity**

said, as she moved her hand to massage the back of her neck. "For me, a neck ache is a sure sign—it's a sure sign I'm over doing."

Wendy went on to explain that her friends and family had also missed her— they didn't understand why she hadn't been returning e-mails and phone calls and why she had stopped going out. "I don't want to go out with my friends when I'm feeling tired and tense," Wendy confessed.

I wrote "neck ache," "not making time for important relationships," and "feeling tired, not rested" as Early Warnings on the downside of Activity.

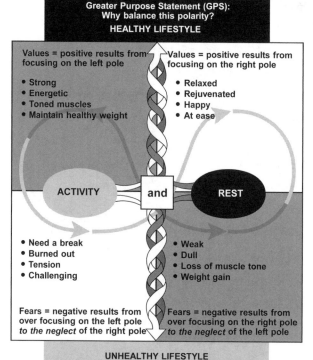

Maintaining a Healthy Lifestyle

Action Steps

How will we gain or maintain the positive results from focusing on this left pole? What? Who? By when? Measures?

Greater Purpose Statement (GPS): Why balance this polarity? HEALTHY LIFESTYLE

Values = positive results from focusing on the left pole

- Strong
- Energetic
- Toned muscles
- Maintain healthy weight

Values = positive results from focusing on the right pole

- Relaxed
- Rejuvenated
- Happy
- At ease

Action Steps

How will we gain or maintain the positive results from focusing on this right pole? What? Who? By when? Measures?

ACTIVITY and **REST**

Early Warnings

Measurable indicators (things you can count) that will let you know that you are getting into the downside of this left pole.

1. Neck ache.
2. Not enough time for important relationships.
3. Feeling tired, not rested.

- Need a break
- Burned out
- Tension
- Challenging

- Weak
- Dull
- Loss of muscle tone
- Weight gain

Early Warnings

Measurable indicators (things you can count) that will let you know that you are getting into the downside of this right pole.

Fears = negative results from over focusing on the left pole *to the neglect* of the right pole

Fears = negative results from over focusing on the right pole *to the neglect* of the left pole

UNHEALTHY LIFESTYLE

Deeper Fear from lack of balance

Polarity Map #8

Following the flow of the Infinity Loop, we moved to the upside of Rest.

"Wendy, what would happen if you knew that the first sign of that neck ache or unanswered e-mail from a friend was an Early Warning for you to take some pressure off and focus on relaxing, resting, and

Action Steps to refocus on Rest

rejuvenating, and that maybe it was time to schedule an outing with a friend or your family members?"

"That," Wendy answered, "would change my life!" She added, "You see, I had a tendency to put off my friends and sometimes even my family because I felt I just couldn't take the time, and I think that actually caused me even more stress. I guess all this is because I was focusing my time and energy on Activity, and was neglecting the positive aspects of Rest."

"You are really getting this!" I commended. "So when this happens, what Action Steps would you take to focus on Rest?"

Wendy was quick to respond: "The first thing I would love to do is to get a full eight hours of sleep. I know my body, and if I'm able to get eight hours, I will feel great the next day. Then I will have the energy to treat myself to dinner with a friend and schedule quality time with the kids."

"That sounds good, but is it doable?" I asked.

Wendy answered, "Yes, it is doable. Once I know what I need to do, I can do it. It's almost like I need to give myself permission." Wendy seemed relieved.

I wrote the Action Steps for Rest in the upper right hand corner of the map.

Maintaining a Healthy Lifestyle

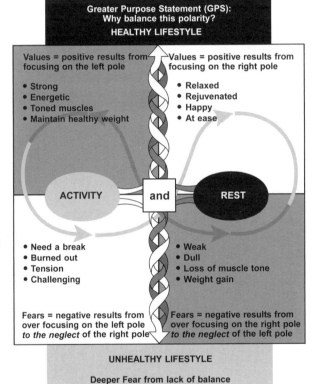

Polarity Map #9

Wendy had picked up on the concepts and terminology of the Polarity Map very quickly. With two more sections of the map to go, I asked, "How will you know you are over focused on Rest to the neglect of Activity? What are the Early Warnings?"

"I think the first warning sign will be that I miss my workouts. I know I'm on the downside of Rest when I'm not exercising, and that's when I would be prone to gaining weight again."

> **Early Warnings due to an over focus on Rest**

"And how many workouts would you miss before you would feel you were on the downside of Rest?" I asked.

Wendy thought this through and concluded that missing one workout a week for a month would be an Early Warning.

"And how many pounds would you feel you could gain before it became an Early Warning?"

Again, Wendy thought and then answered carefully, "Four or five pounds."

I filled in the Early Warnings of over focus on Rest to the neglect of Activity.

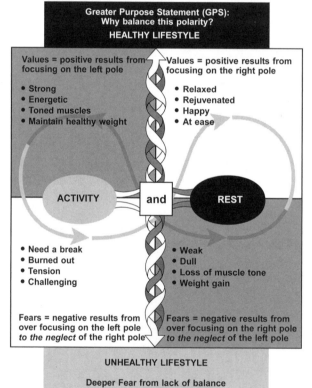

Maintaining a Healthy Lifestyle

Action Steps

How will we gain or maintain the positive results from focusing on this left pole? What? Who? By when? Measures?

Greater Purpose Statement (GPS): Why balance this polarity?
HEALTHY LIFESTYLE

Values = positive results from focusing on the left pole

- Strong
- Energetic
- Toned muscles
- Maintain healthy weight

Values = positive results from focusing on the right pole

- Relaxed
- Rejuvenated
- Happy
- At ease

Action Steps

How will we gain or maintain the positive results from focusing on this right pole? What? Who? By when? Measures?

1. Eight hours of rest.
2. Dinner out with friends.
3. Schedule quality family time.

ACTIVITY **and** REST

Early Warnings

Measurable indicators (things you can count) that will let you know that you are getting into the downside of this left pole.

- Need a break
- Burned out
- Tension
- Challenging

- Weak
- Dull
- Loss of muscle tone
- Weight gain

Early Warnings

Measurable indicators (things you can count) that will let you know that you are getting into the downside of this right pole.

1. Neck ache.
2. Not enough time for important relationships.
3. Feeling tired, not rested.

Fears = negative results from over focusing on the left pole *to the neglect* of the right pole

Fears = negative results from over focusing on the right pole *to the neglect* of the left pole

1. Miss one workout each week for a month.
2. A weight gain of 4 or 5 pounds.

UNHEALTHY LIFESTYLE

Deeper Fear from lack of balance

Polarity Map #10

And finally, I asked Wendy, "What Action Steps will you take to achieve the upside of Activity?"

Wendy was cautious; she wanted to get back to the five workouts a week, but now she could see that was unrealistic if she were to have time to balance both Activity and Rest. She needed to reduce her time on the Activity side of her map in order to have the time to be successful on the Rest side of her map.

> **Action Steps to refocus on Activity**

"I'll cut back to four days of activity a week. I could go to the club three times a week and schedule an outdoor event on Saturday with my kids to get in that fourth activity," she said. That will free up some time and incorporate a date with my kids, and exercising together will be good for them, too."

I filled in the final set of Action Steps and turned the map for Wendy to read.

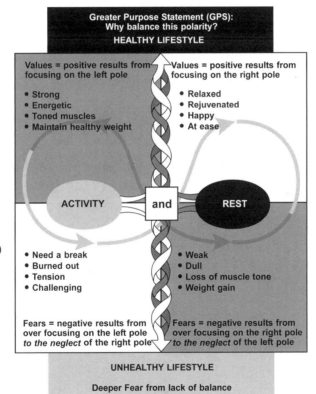

Maintaining a Healthy Lifestyle

Action Steps

How will we gain or maintain the positive results from focusing on this left pole? What? Who? By when? Measures?

1. Exercise three times a week at the club.
2. Saturday activity with the kids.

Action Steps

How will we gain or maintain the positive results from focusing on this right pole? What? Who? By when? Measures?

1. Eight hours of rest.
2. Dinner out with friends.
3. Schedule quality family time.

Greater Purpose Statement (GPS): Why balance this polarity?
HEALTHY LIFESTYLE

Values = positive results from focusing on the left pole
- Strong
- Energetic
- Toned muscles
- Maintain healthy weight

Values = positive results from focusing on the right pole
- Relaxed
- Rejuvenated
- Happy
- At ease

ACTIVITY and **REST**

Early Warnings

Measurable indicators (things you can count) that will let you know that you are getting into the downside of this left pole.

1. Neck ache.
2. Not enough time for important relationships.
3. Feeling tired, not rested.

- Need a break
- Burned out
- Tension
- Challenging

- Weak
- Dull
- Loss of muscle tone
- Weight gain

Early Warnings

Measurable indicators (things you can count) that will let you know that you are getting into the downside of this right pole.

1. Miss one workout each week for a month.
2. A weight gain of 4 or 5 pounds.

Fears = negative results from over focusing on the left pole *to the neglect* of the right pole

Fears = negative results from over focusing on the right pole *to the neglect* of the left pole

UNHEALTHY LIFESTYLE

Deeper Fear from lack of balance

Polarity Map #11

As we looked at the completed map, I felt some apprehension on Wendy's part. I asked if I was accurate in sensing her apprehension.

"I am concerned that my Action Steps for activity are too much. I want to exercise four times a week. I really don't want to cut back on that any further, but

I'm concerned about the time commitment given the time I need to focus on my Action Steps for rest," Wendy answered. "I want this to be doable."

"Let's look at that more closely. I'm hearing you say you want the four times a week to stay the same—that that's an important goal. So what about that four times a week could be different? What could be different and still get in your four activities per week while maintaining your goals for Activity and Rest?" I asked.

Wendy thought for a moment and then said eagerly, "I've got it! It's not the time for my workout, it's the drive time that could be saved. I'd love to free up some of that drive time to and from the club. To do that, I will exercise at home once a week. I'll still get my workout in, but I'll be saving the drive time and the gas as well—a side benefit! Besides, my trainer has advised me to switch up my exercise routines, and I know I have an old 'Buns of Steel' video somewhere in my basement," Wendy smiled.

I changed three times a week at the club to two times, and added "Buns of Steel" to the Action Steps for Activity.

Maintaining a Healthy Lifestyle

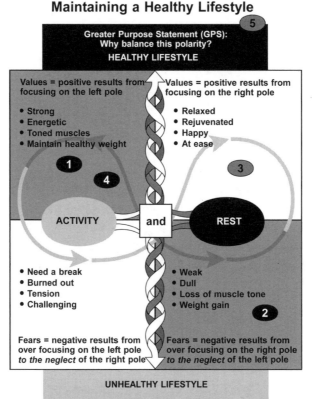

Polarity Map #12

"I can't believe it!" Wendy smiled. "I can see exactly why I got stuck. Without your coaching and this Polarity Map I would not have been able to see the positive aspects of Rest. I would have focused only on Activity as the answer to a healthy lifestyle and I would have been back where I started in a few short months. I'm going to use this map to explain to my family what my Activity and Rest goals are, the changes in my workout routine, and how my priorities include time with them as a family. I need their understanding and support and this map will be easy for them to understand. Using this map I can see what I need to do in order to meet and maintain my Healthy Lifestyle!"

"Thanks, Coach!" Wendy said sincerely as she got up to leave. "I'll see you next week."

~

Wendy saw her issue as a problem to solve. Blind to the value of the interdependent pole, she was on her way to repeating a pattern that had not produced the results she had hoped for. It was clearly an over focus on Activity that led her to experience of the downside of both poles.

The Getting Unstuck Model helps the client move from "either/or" thinking to "both/and" thinking and is an example of what Dr. Barry Johnson refers to as a "flip" in poles. When you over focus on one pole to the sustained neglect of the other, first you get the downside of the pole on which you over focus, then you get the downside of the interdependent pole as well. Ironically, you get what you are attempting to avoid.

Wendy's case is a great example of getting the downside of the less preferred pole through an over focus on the preferred pole. With Polarity Coaching, Wendy was able to affirm and gain the upside of Rest in order to supplement that with her goal: a return to the club and ultimately a healthy lifestyle. Wendy was able to realize the value of Rest and its benefits to attaining and maintaining her Greater Purpose.

The Getting Unstuck™ Model is a tool for every coach's toolkit to help the client find the value of what he or she may see as an opposing view, rather than an interdependent pole.

~

Next we see how words can result in unintended impact and how understanding another person's preferred pole can help understand and soften the emotional reaction of those words and strengthen the conversation. For Donna, being aware that she had to embrace her daughter's preferred pole opened new possibilities that helped shift a negative experience into something more positive.

Case Study #6
Gentle Love and Tough Love

There is one thing nearly all parents would agree on and that is that raising children can be a challenge. I know I was a challenge for my parents, and while raising my own children I knew what "pay-back time" meant.

My coaching client, Donna, also knew what it meant to be challenged as a parent, especially by her daughter Megan. Donna had been married for five years when her first marriage ended. She was a single mom of two, Tim the oldest and Megan three years younger, when she met and married Mike. As in many blended families, the majority of the parenting was Donna's responsibility; she knew she had Mike's love and support, but the day-to-day discipline of the children, then 13 and 10 years old, was hers.

Donna had hired me off and on to coach her through the many issues and opportunities of a blended family. Tim, now 19, had done very well throughout high school and was in his first year at the University. Megan, 16, had always been her "strong-willed" child: bright, assertive, and self-confident. In many ways, Megan's assertive personality and assured demeanor were positive qualities, and Donna did not want to squelch Megan's confidence. Yet these qualities also came across as arrogant and were unpredictable. When Megan wanted something, she took control of the conversation. She would not listen to Donna and would often argue her point until Donna would give in from sheer weariness. Life seemed to be a continuous struggle when it came to parenting Megan. Now, as we began our coaching call, Donna told me how things had escalated since our last session.

"It's been a very difficult week, Coach," Donna said with a sad voice. "I received a call from one of Megan's teachers that her grades have fallen off, and yesterday she stayed out past her curfew again. I was in the kitchen when she came home from school today. I felt a bit uneasy because I knew she would come in the kitchen to get something to eat, and I knew I had to talk with her about being out past curfew. So she came in, I asked her about coming in late, and she gave me a curt response and brushed me off. I started to tell her that her teacher had called, but rather than listening to me, she stormed out of the kitchen."

I sensed Donna was almost ready to cry, but she continued to talk.

"I didn't know raising a teenager could be this hard. I have tried to be flexible and understanding, yet I always end up feeling manipulated by my own daughter. And as I reflect on the past two weeks, I have a feeling Megan has been lying to me about what she's been doing and whom she's been spending her time with. This really hurts and it's getting out of hand—lying is simply unacceptable to me," Donna lamented.

Donna continued to reveal her feelings, "I have tried to talk with her about my concerns; I very gently try to engage her in conversation to let her know how much I love her and that I understand she's going through many emotional and even hormonal changes right now. I want her to know she's loved unconditionally, yet I don't feel a sense of respect. In fact, it's just the opposite—her typical response is to ignore me—you know, tune me out. One time I had had enough and I tried to confront her about her attitude."

"How did Megan respond to that?" I asked curiously.

"I guess she saw it coming, and she blew up before I could finish. She called me a dictator! I was so taken aback I had to leave the room so that she wouldn't see how hurt I was by that comment. I was very hurt! I can see that my approach is not helping our relationship, but I don't know what else to do," Donna said in a desperate voice.

My heart went out to Donna. I looked at the list I had made as she talked:

Donna	Megan
flexible	bright, strong-willed
understanding	arrogant, unpredictable
manipulated	controlling
hurt	argumentative
loving	brush off/tune out (dismissive)

Over the years, I have come to know Donna as a gentle and loving person. I knew she was driven by a motivational value that led her thoughts and actions; I called that value gentle love. She wanted to be the best mom she could possibly be, and she believed the best way to parent was to practice gentle love. Unfortunately, gentle love alone was ineffective with Megan, and looking only from that value, she would continue to experience problems and be manipulated by Megan. I believed that the interdependent value—tough love—was needed to provide balance and improve the relationship.

"Donna, we've used a Polarity Map in the past, and it has helped us look at the positive aspects of a given situation, as well as the consequences. I think it could be helpful here," I suggested.

"Of course," Donna replied. "That's a great idea!"

"Okay, do you have a piece of paper handy?" I asked.

Because we had coached using a Polarity Map before, Donna was familiar with the layout and the terminology of Polarity Management. I suggested we each draw a map and work together to fill it in.

"Remember to write the word 'and' in the center box. The 'and' is our cue that the two sides of the map are interdependent; both sides work together to provide balance."

"Yes," Donna answered. "I remember. Both sides are true, but standing alone they represent only half of the picture, only half of the truth."

"That's right. You understand this very well, Donna," I said confirming her explanation.

We drew our maps.

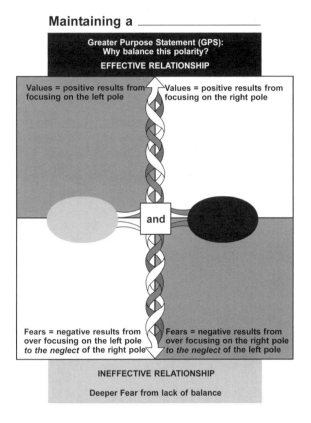

Maintaining a _____

Greater Purpose Statement (GPS):
Why balance this polarity?
EFFECTIVE RELATIONSHIP

Values = positive results from focusing on the left pole | Values = positive results from focusing on the right pole

and

Fears = negative results from over focusing on the left pole *to the neglect* of the right pole | Fears = negative results from over focusing on the right pole *to the neglect* of the left pole

INEFFECTIVE RELATIONSHIP

Deeper Fear from lack of balance

Polarity Map #1

With maps in front of us, Donna started, "I'm looking at my empty map, and I have no idea where to begin."

"Let's begin with the Greater Purpose," I suggested. "The Greater Purpose is what you are hoping for. What are you hoping for, Donna?" I asked.

"I'm hoping for a lot of things," Donna said quickly. "I'm hoping to feel less frustrated, and I'm hoping for a better relationship with Megan; a relationship based on honest communication—honest communication is very important to me. I also want her to recognize that I love

Greater Purpose

her and that I want to be there for her in an honest and open way without feeling on guard, like I'm being manipulated or dismissed. I want her to be happy and successful in school, and I hope to get past these teenage years in one piece!" she concluded with a bit of levity.

"Good! So if you could boil all that down into a few words, what would they be?" I asked.

"Ummm," Donna hesitated. "I think I would say an 'honest, effective relationship with my daughter.'"

"Okay, let's write 'Honest, Effective Relationship' in the Greater Purpose box at the top of the map. Now the bottom box, the Deeper Fear—what do you want to avoid at all costs?" I continued.

"I want to avoid a stressful, unpredictable relationship that consists of arguing rather than meaningful conversation," Donna replied. "And no more lies."

"Yes," I affirmed. "It sounds like that boils down to a dishonest, ineffective relationship."

Donna thought a moment and then added, "I think it's simpler than that. To me, honesty is inherent in an effective relationship, just as dishonesty is

Deeper Fear

usually part of an ineffective relationship. Yes, it seems simple—the Greater Purpose is effective relationship, and the Deeper Fear is ineffective relationship."

"Okay," I said, affirming Donna's clarity.

We both penciled "Effective Relationship" as the Greater Purpose in the top box of the map, and "Ineffective Relationship" as the Deeper Fear in the box at the bottom of the map.

"Let's draw in the upward and downward spirals, the Virtuous and Vicious cycles," I suggested.

"Can you review that again for me, Kathy?" Donna asked. "I know where to put the spirals, but I need a review on what it means."

"Sure," I replied. "The upward spiral, called the Virtuous Cycle, exists when the motivational values, or poles on the Polarity Map, work in concert and support to attain the Greater Purpose—when the val-

Virtuous and Vicious Cycles

ues are in balance with one another. The downward spiral, or Vicious Cycle, is created from the negative results of over focus on one pole or value, to the neglect of the other interdependent pole or value. You can think of it as a conflict between the two poles."

"Okay, I remember now," Donna said thoughtfully. "I'm feeling the movement on the downward spiral in my relationship with Megan right now, and with the Polarity Map, I can identify what I need to do to gain balance and create upward movement toward the Greater Purpose."

"Exactly," I confirmed. "Now let's name the poles. Donna, I know you love Megan and that you want an effective relationship. I'm hearing you say that you have been striving to be flexible and understanding toward Megan."

"Yes, and I'm trying to communicate with her in a very caring and loving way," Donna responded.

"Do the words 'gentle love' resonate with you?" I asked.

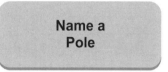

Donna thought for a moment and then responded slowly. "Yes, they do—I like that. I'm a pretty calm and gentle person by nature."

"So, if Gentle Love is our left pole, the right pole would be…" I waited for Donna to finish my sentence.

"Ah," Donna said slowly, "I guess it would be Tough Love—I'm not very good at that. For me, tough love generates negative pictures of the dictator Megan accused me of being, and that is not my idea of an effective relationship."

"There is a downside to Tough Love, just as there is a downside to Gentle Love," I added. "Let's start here, and if we find something that fits better, we can adjust."

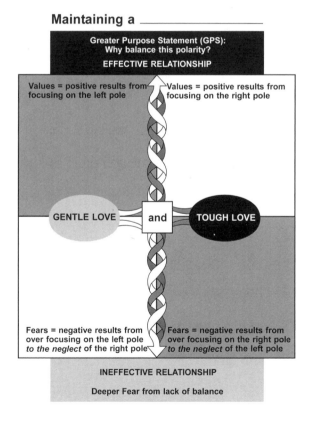

Polarity Map #2

Donna sighed, "Okay, this looks hard, but let's work the map, Coach."

"Let's start in the upper left quadrant, the positive results, or upside, of Gentle Love," I continued, "What values live in Gentle Love.

Upper Left Quadrant for Gentle Love

"Good," Donna answered. "That's easy for me. The values I hold here are to have a caring and loving relationship."

I could see that a caring and loving relationship was possible through Tough Love as well, but I knew I needed to use my client's language and what made sense to her personally, so I decided not to question Donna's view.

"Let's write "Caring and loving" in the upper left quadrant," I proposed. "What else?"

"I'm not sure," Donna answered thoughtfully.

After a moment of silence, I noted, "I heard you describe yourself as flexible and understanding. Does that have a place on the map?" I asked.

"Yes," Donna agreed. "I think part of gentle love is being flexible and understanding, but they are not connected. What I mean is a person can be flexible and not understand or care about what they are being flexible about. And a person can understand what is desired, but be inflexible. I see them as two separate character traits of gentle love. I like to be flexible, and I want to understand why I'm being flexible."

"Nice distinction—so in the upside of Gentle Love we have "Caring and loving" on one line, followed by "Flexible," and under that is "Understanding," I confirmed.

Donna agreed, "That's what I have."

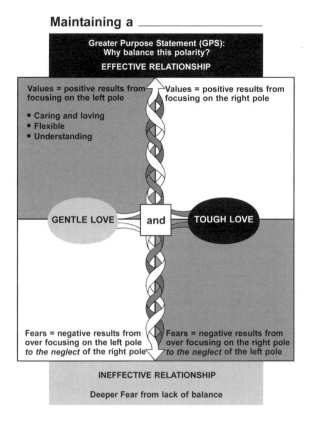

Maintaining a _____

> **Greater Purpose Statement (GPS):**
> **Why balance this polarity?**
> **EFFECTIVE RELATIONSHIP**

Values = positive results from focusing on the left pole

- Caring and loving
- Flexible
- Understanding

Values = positive results from focusing on the right pole

GENTLE LOVE — and — **TOUGH LOVE**

Fears = negative results from over focusing on the left pole *to the neglect* of the right pole

Fears = negative results from over focusing on the right pole *to the neglect* of the left pole

INEFFECTIVE RELATIONSHIP

Deeper Fear from lack of balance

Polarity Map #3

"Oh," Donna said slowly. "I know what comes next."

"Yes, the downside of Gentle Love," I answered. "While you have been operating out of your natural value of Gentle Love, there have been some negative results. Are you ready to explore that?"

> **Lower Left Quadrant for Gentle Love**

"Yes, let's do it," Donna said a little reluctantly.

"Okay. Donna, I heard you say you felt manipulated. Is that true?" I asked.

"Yes, I hate to admit it," Donna confessed. "Megan is very smart, and I love that about her, and she is also strong willed. But I feel that she manipulates me to get her way. And when I'm honest with myself, I've made it easy for her. I haven't set the boundaries I should have set, and I haven't enforced consequences or called her on her manipulative behavior. I can see that now."

"So would you say a downside of gentle love is being easily manipulated?" I asked.

"Yes, I have to admit that is probably true," Donna responded.

"What else?" I asked.

"Well, Megan can be very assertive, even aggressive. She will argue a point on something, and pretty soon I feel like I'm the daughter and she's the mother," Donna confessed with a loud sigh. "She's a lot like her father that way."

That was a significant statement—it took a lot of courage for Donna to verbalize the similarity between her ex-husband's personality and Megan's. I let the comment land in its proper place for Donna, as together we found relief in a moment of silence.

Then Donna continued, "I think perhaps Megan has a very different natural set of values than I do. Looking at it from a polarity perspective, I think perhaps Megan's natural bias is Tough Love. I feel I may have been unable to recognize that Megan needs a very different response from me than I have been giving her. If Megan's preferred pole is Tough Love, and I've been giving her Gentle Love, that may be why I feel she has lost respect for me and knows that she can manipulate me."

"Let me think a moment," said Donna, hesitating a moment before slowly beginning again. "If this is true, and if I step back and look at this from Megan's natural value—her preference for Tough Love—then what she sees is the downside of Gentle Love, right Coach? She sees me as soft and wishy-washy, someone she can easily manipulate. Wow—this is really shifting my paradigm!" Donna announced.

"That's a lot to unpack in a short time," I cautioned, "but I think you are definitely onto something."

"Oh, yes," Donna responded. "This picture is unfolding. The upside of Gentle Love is caring and loving, understanding, and flexibility. Megan isn't at a point in her life where she can respect my approach, so what she sees in me is the downside of Gentle Love. She sees someone she can easily manipulate to get what she wants, someone who is soft and wishy-washy, and she's right. I haven't called her on the manipulation, I've let her have her way far too often, and even when I take a stand on something, I back down to her persistent arguments. I can see this now. Megan doesn't naturally value Gentle Love and so she doesn't respect my approach," she said again slowly as if to really absorb what she had said.

There was a silence to let this heavy reality sink in.

"What's next?" I asked softly, breaking the silence.

"I'm filling in the downside of Gentle Love. I have written 'Easily manipulated,' 'Soft,' and 'Wishy-washy.' Yuk, I really don't like that, but it's true!" Donna stated.

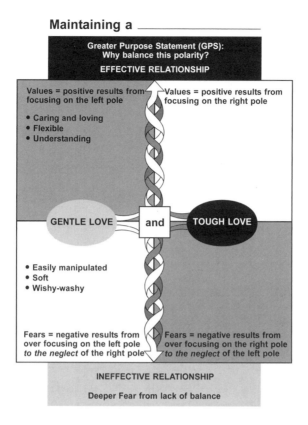

Polarity Map #4

Donna seemed to have a renewed energy as she took hold of the coaching conversation. "I'm looking at our situation in a whole new light," she said. "I can see now how our different values have contributed to our difficulties. I want to define my Tough Love role for Megan."

"Define your Tough Love role for Megan?" I questioned. "What are you seeing?"

Donna went on. "If Megan's natural value is Tough Love, then I'll parent from the Tough Love pole. She will pick up on that and will no longer see me as soft and wishy-washy."

I knew Donna was experiencing the downside of Gentle Love and now saw Tough Love as the solution to the situation. In this case I was seeing Gentle Love and Tough Love as interdependent pairs. I wanted to tell her that seeing Tough Love as the solution to the issue and rushing to Tough Love would only result in the downside of Tough Love, but I decided to hold back on that for now and keep working the map.

"I know there is truth in that statement, Donna, and I'm getting the sense that you've already started making some conclusions; however, to get the full picture, let's work through the map and see what else pops out," I said hoping to keep the focus on the Polarity Map. "So standing in the Tough Love perspective, let's look at the upside of tough love. Can you put yourself in that place?" I asked.

> **Upper Right Quadrant for Tough Love**

"Well, yes, this is where I need to stand. Even though that's not my natural pole, I think that Megan would feel that coming from a position of Tough Love would be coming from a position of strength, you know, as opposed to soft and wishy-washy," Donna said, feeling sure of herself.

"Okay. What do you mean by 'position of strength'?" I asked.

Thinking a moment before speaking, Donna then went on, "I see that I could confront her lies. By that I mean to frame my conversation from a position of strength, not in anger or frustration as I talked about earlier."

"Okay. Do you see that that is possible for you?" I asked.

"Yes, it has to be," Donna answered quickly and firmly. "Let's write 'Confronting deception' in the upper right quadrant," she said.

"Okay, what else?" I asked.

"I need to be clear about the rules and enforce the rules—I need to hold her accountable. And I need to be clear about the consequence of breaking the rules, like curfew. I've been approaching the rules from a gentle-love value bias, and I can see now that doesn't work for Megan. Tough love comes from a position of boundaries and accountability—from a position of strict compliance to the rules," Donna clarified.

"Right," I affirmed. "So we have 'Confronting deception,' 'Be clear about the rules,' 'Hold accountable.'"

"Yes," Donna said confidently, "that will work."

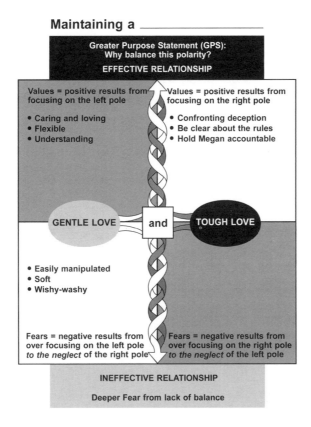

Maintaining a _____

Greater Purpose Statement (GPS):
Why balance this polarity?
EFFECTIVE RELATIONSHIP

Values = positive results from focusing on the left pole

- Caring and loving
- Flexible
- Understanding

Values = positive results from focusing on the right pole

- Confronting deception
- Be clear about the rules
- Hold Megan accountable

GENTLE LOVE and **TOUGH LOVE**

- Easily manipulated
- Soft
- Wishy-washy

Fears = negative results from over focusing on the left pole *to the neglect* of the right pole

Fears = negative results from over focusing on the right pole *to the neglect* of the left pole

INEFFECTIVE RELATIONSHIP

Deeper Fear from lack of balance

Polarity Map #5

"Now, one more quadrant, Donna, the downside of Tough Love," I added.

"Oh, and I was just seeing the virtue of Tough Love," Donna said laughing. "Seriously, though, I have always feared the downside of Tough Love. Remember when I said Megan called me a dictator? To me, dictator is on the downside of Tough Love. I think of a cruel, insensitive dictator of a parent."

"Yes, you said you were very hurt by that, when Megan called you a dictator," I recalled.

"Yes, very hurt!" Donna confirmed.

"So in the downside of Tough Love I have 'Cruel,' 'Insensitive,' and 'Dictator.' What do you think?" I said.

> **Lower Right Quadrant**
> **For Tough Love**

"Yes, that's it," Donna answered.

"Are you comfortable with the map so far, Donna?" I asked.

"Yes, it's good," Donna answered.

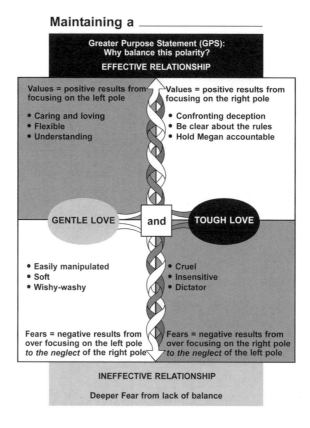

Maintaining a _____

Greater Purpose Statement (GPS):
Why balance this polarity?
EFFECTIVE RELATIONSHIP

Values = positive results from focusing on the left pole

• Caring and loving
• Flexible
• Understanding

Values = positive results from focusing on the right pole

• Confronting deception
• Be clear about the rules
• Hold Megan accountable

GENTLE LOVE   and   TOUGH LOVE

• Easily manipulated
• Soft
• Wishy-washy

• Cruel
• Insensitive
• Dictator

Fears = negative results from over focusing on the left pole *to the neglect* of the right pole

Fears = negative results from over focusing on the right pole *to the neglect* of the left pole

INEFFECTIVE RELATIONSHIP

Deeper Fear from lack of balance

Polarity Map #6

Now was the time to drop in the Infinity Loop.

"Great," I noted. "We now have the whole picture of Gentle Love and Tough Love, and walking through the Polarity Map, we can see the upside of Gentle Love, the downside of Gentle Love, the upside of Tough Love, and finally the downside of Tough Love. To show that more clearly, let's draw in the Infinity Loop."

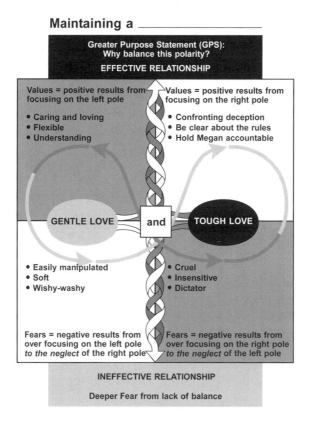

Maintaining a _____

Greater Purpose Statement (GPS):
Why balance this polarity?
EFFECTIVE RELATIONSHIP

Values = positive results from
focusing on the left pole

- Caring and loving
- Flexible
- Understanding

Values = positive results from
focusing on the right pole

- Confronting deception
- Be clear about the rules
- Hold Megan accountable

GENTLE LOVE and **TOUGH LOVE**

- Easily manipulated
- Soft
- Wishy-washy

- Cruel
- Insensitive
- Dictator

Fears = negative results from
over focusing on the left pole
to the neglect of the right pole

Fears = negative results from
over focusing on the right pole
to the neglect of the left pole

INEFFECTIVE RELATIONSHIP

Deeper Fear from lack of balance

Polarity Map #7

"Now, let's review by following the flow of the Infinity Loop," I continued. "The Infinity Loop reminds us that the two values are interdependent; they are connected. Let's start with Gentle Love. Tell

Infinity Loop

me what happens when you over focus on Gentle Love to the neglect of Tough Love."

Donna answered, "I think that's what has been happening. I feel I'm being caring and loving, but Megan doesn't see that. She sees someone who can be easily manipulated; she sees me as soft and wishy-washy. So my natural tendency to over focus on Gentle Love has brought us to the downside of Gentle Love."

"Yes," I affirmed. "So you are living in the downside of Gentle Love. What's next?"

"Okay," Donna thought a moment. "I'm glad I've been through this before, because this part is difficult. Let me think. Being in the downside of Gentle Love means I naturally want to rush to Tough Love. I'm also seeing now that tough love is Megan's natural tendency and I want to align with her and focus on Tough Love, hoping that will improve our situation. However, if I follow the Infinity Loop, my move to the upside of Tough Love, to the neglect of Gentle

Love, it will bring us to the downside of Tough Love," Donna said slowly and thoughtfully.

Donna saw what I was hoping she'd see; she saw the whole picture with both poles at work. "Good, really good," I affirmed. "It's important to understand that over focus on Tough Love to the neglect of Gentle Love will simply create another set of problems."

"Yes, and my natural bias dislikes Tough Love and I can easily see the downside of Tough Love," Donna said firmly.

"Do you think Megan felt I was moving to Tough Love when she called me a dictator?" Donna questioned.

"Perhaps," I replied. "What do you think?"

"It was out of character for me to confront her the way I did, and Megan resisted it. Our conversation moved quickly to the downside of Tough Love." Donna's voice got quiet as she recalled the argument and the distress of that moment.

"So what's the answer, Donna?" I asked thoughtfully.

"The gentle parenting style alone is clearly not working, and my relationship with Megan continues to worsen," Donna said. "I can also see that a shift to Tough Love will simply create a different set of problems. I need to intentionally look for the right balance in parenting Megan. I need to follow the Infinity Loop and balance Gentle Love and Tough Love. Both poles are important, and I need both to reach the Greater Purpose, an effective relationship with my daughter."

"Yes, both are needed," I acknowledged.

"This will be hard to do," Donna said with a sigh.

"Let's add Action Steps and Early Warnings. Action Steps and Early Warnings will make it easier by helping to identify how and when to use the interdependent poles creating the balance you need," I encouraged.

"I need all the help I can get," Donna stated. "I'm expanding my map to include the space for Action Steps and Early Warnings."

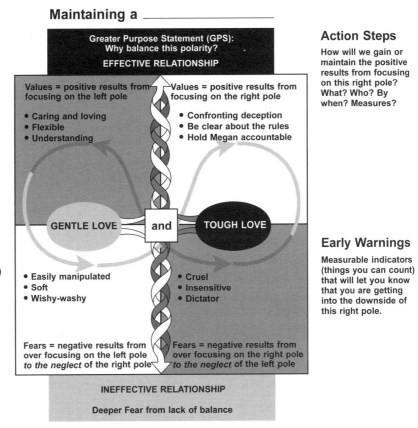

Maintaining a _____

Polarity Map #8

I've done the same. "Are you ready to fill this part in, Donna?" I asked.

"Yes, let's do it," Donna said with renewed enthusiasm.

"Great. Let's begin by looking at Early Warnings of Gentle Love. What Early Warnings have you been getting from Megan that tell you that you've over focused on Gentle Love?" I asked.

"She has no interest in talking with me. It's clear she deliberately tunes me out," Donna answered.

"Okay. That's one," I said as I wrote. "What else?"

> **Early Warnings due to an over focus on Gentle Love**

"She stays out past curfew and either shrugs it off or makes a lame excuse, an excuse she knows I'm going to see right through. The fact that I'm her mother doesn't seem to matter; she acts like she doesn't even care about our relationship," Donna said.

"Okay, so Megan breaks the rules, you feel disrespected, and Megan appears cold and uncaring about your relationship as mother and daughter."

"Yes," Donna said. "That about sums it up."

"So in the Early Warning box next to Gentle Love, the first Early Warning is, 'Tunes me out,' next, 'Breaks the rules,' third, 'Shows disrespect,' and fourth, 'Acts cold and uncaring.' I've got that written in," I confirmed.

"Yes. I have that too," Donna responded. "It's all too familiar." She said sadly.

Maintaining a _____

Action Steps

How will we gain or maintain the positive results from focusing on this left pole? What? Who? By when? Measures?

Greater Purpose Statement (GPS): Why balance this polarity?
EFFECTIVE RELATIONSHIP

Values = positive results from focusing on the left pole

- Caring and loving
- Flexible
- Understanding

Values = positive results from focusing on the right pole

- Confronting deception
- Be clear about the rules
- Hold Megan accountable

Action Steps

How will we gain or maintain the positive results from focusing on this right pole? What? Who? By when? Measures?

GENTLE LOVE and **TOUGH LOVE**

Early Warnings

Measurable indicators (things you can count) that will let you know that you are getting into the downside of this left pole.

1. Tunes me out.
2. Breaks the rules.
3. Shows disrepect.
4. Acts cold and uncaring.

- Easily manipulated
- Soft
- Wishy-washy

- Cruel
- Insensitive
- Dictator

Early Warnings

Measurable indicators (things you can count) that will let you know that you are getting into the downside of this right pole.

Fears = negative results from over focusing on the left pole *to the neglect* of the right pole

Fears = negative results from over focusing on the right pole *to the neglect* of the left pole

INEFFECTIVE RELATIONSHIP

Deeper Fear from lack of balance

Polarity Map #9

"So as we discussed earlier, when you are experiencing all this, you realize your motivational value, which is Gentle Love, is not working," I stated.

"Yes, that's right," Donna replied.

"Okay, now what are some Action Steps you can take that will help you move to the upside of Tough Love?" I asked.

"I need to be calm, not frustrated, and I need to be direct, but not confrontational," Donna said thoughtfully.

Action Steps to refocus on Tough Love

"Good," I replied. I've written in 'Calm and direct.' What's next?"

112

Donna added, "I need to parent in an assertive way. Megan speaks assertively, and I think she respects that type of conversation. Her natural tendency is to argue and debate, and I can't give in to her—I need to match her behavior in a calm, direct, and respectful way; I need to be up to the challenge of debating back. And I have to set reasonable expectations and communicate and enforce consequences when the expectations are not met," Donna continued.

"Okay. I've written the first action step as 'Calm and direct;' action step number two, 'Be assertive and debate respectfully;' action step number three, 'Communicate reasonable expectations and consequences;' and the last one is 'Enforce consequences.' How's that?" I inquired.

"Yes," Donna responded, "and there is one more thing. I need to know Megan understands the expectations and the consequences. She may not agree, but this won't work unless I know she understands them."

"Sounds good," I affirmed. "How about 'Expectations and consequences are understood' as number four, and 'Enforce consequences' as number five.

"Yes, that's good," Donna said with a sigh of relief. "I'm feeling stronger already!"

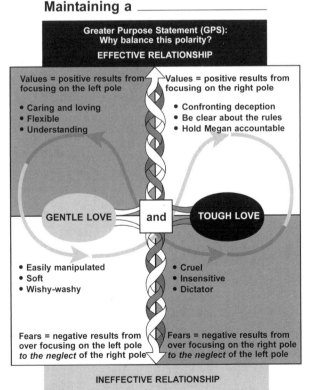

Polarity Map #10

"Now, Donna," I cautioned. "How will you know when Tough Love isn't working?"

"Ah," Donna said lightly. "You mean when my daughter calls me a dictator, and I leave the room ready to burst into tears?"

"Yes, that would be it," I said as we both giggled a bit trying to add some levity to this serious conversation.

"Seriously, though," Donna said quickly. "Perhaps it's when we reach a stalemate—you know, my rules are on the table, and there is no more conversation. When this happens, she is likely to break the rules in defiance."

> **Early Warnings due to an over focus on Tough Love**

"Okay," I said. "Rules stifle communication. Why would the rules stifle communication?"

"Megan says my rules are too restrictive and the consequences too harsh," Donna responded.

"Are they?" I asked.

"I don't think they are, but if Megan does, then the rules aren't going to work, are they?" Donna said slowly.

"As a parent, you have a right to set the rules you feel are appropriate to set," I said as I put some of our relational capital on the line.

"Yes, I realize that," Donna answered. "At the same time, Megan is a strong-willed child, and if the rules aren't meaningful to Megan, if she feels the rules are one-sided, her assertive nature will push back, and she won't comply with them."

"So what's the Early Warning in all of this?" I asked.

Donna responded slowly, "If I outline the rules, with curfew for example, and Megan doesn't agree, she'll simply ignore the rules. I guess the Early Warning is Megan ignores the rules."

"Okay, the rules are ignored. What else?" I asked.

"No communication," Donna acknowledged. "When there is no communication."

"Yes," I agreed. "Any others?"

"Those are the two biggest Early Warnings," Donna answered with some uncertainty.

"Are you a little hesitant?" I questioned.

"Well," Donna continued, "This is where I think I feel like giving up. I hate to say it, but when Megan breaks the rules repeatedly, I feel like giving up, and I'd like to add that as another downside of Tough Love. Tough Love is not my natural tendency, so when I'm not seeing results, in fact seeing resistance, it's hard for me to hang onto the Tough Love pole."

"That makes sense," I responded, as I added those words.

Together we reviewed the Action Steps and Early Warnings of being over focused on Tough Love.

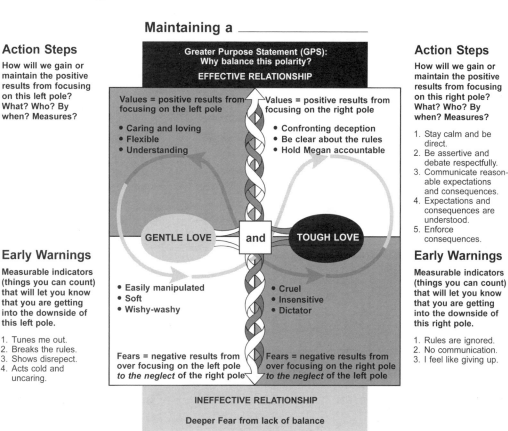

Polarity Map #11

"Our final step, Donna, if you begin to see the Early Warnings of Tough Love, what Gentle Love Action Steps need to be taken?" I inquired.

"If I find myself in the downside of Tough Love, I think I need to step back and take a breath, because I'm probably ready to give up, and that would lead down the vicious cycle once again. I think I would need to calmly listen to Megan's point of view and decide if I can change my position to get closer to what she's looking for without compromising what I know, as her mother, is right for her. I know we won't always agree, and that's okay, but I have to explain that as her mom I am responsible for her, and I'm doing the best job I can because I love her," Donna said gently, but firmly.

Action Steps to refocus on Gentle Love

"Here's what I heard, Donna," I said to clarify. "You want to first, step back and breathe; second, listen; third, revise your position if that's possible for you to do; fourth, explain your responsibilities as Megan's mother; and fifth, express your love."

"Yes," Donna agreed. "That sounds really good. Oh, and one more thing."

"Sure, what else?" I questioned.

"I'd like to call this map 'Maintaining a Love Balance.' That's what this is all about; it's about maintaining a love balance with my daughter."

> Name the Map

We both added those words to the top of the map and paused to view the complete Polarity Map.

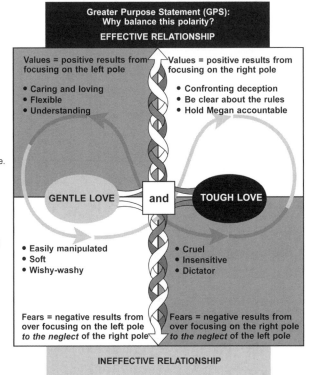

Maintaining a Love Balance

Polarity Map #12

As we closed our session for the day, Donna acknowledged how helpful the Polarity Map exercise had been. I knew Donna felt good about the progress we had made, and I was glad that the map helped her understand the dynamics at work between her and her daughter.

During the week that followed, Donna e-mailed me to let me know she was working hard to balance Gentle Love and Tough Love, watching for the Early Warnings and taking the Action Steps we had outlined.

The day came for our next call, and I was curious about how Donna's week had been.

Now as we began our coaching session, Donna jumped in and exclaimed, "It's been a very good week, Coach!"

~

Donna and her daughter have different personalities and different preferred poles. Polarity Management helped Donna understand that her natural tendency was not working with her strong-willed child. When Donna began to recognize her daughter's preferred pole, she was able to utilize the value of that pole to communicate her expectations in a healthy way. Donna discovered that "both/and" thinking as a supplement to "either/or" thinking was the right balance.

~

The final case demonstrates that too much of a good thing can create an unbalanced life. Polarity Management helped Sarah see this before she gave up on her dream.

Case Study #7
Caring for Self and
Caring for Customers

Sarah had worked at what some might call a cushy government job for 15 years. The first years had been exciting and fresh as she learned and grew in her job. She was committed to the job and didn't mind putting in extra hours that were often needed to finish a project, even when it meant sacrificing personal time and cancelling plans. Sarah had energy and drive and did what it took to achieve excellence. Her work was acknowledged, and she was promoted. She met her new responsibilities with hard work and made many significant contributions to her division. She was satisfied with her work and happy to know she had a secure job.

Then something changed; it was almost like someone flipped a switch. She became bored and no longer felt challenged. She dreaded walking through the doors to the office and would get headaches almost every day of the week. Her energy turned negative, and working the 40 hours each week was almost unbearable.

She confided in a close friend about her feelings. The friend spoke frankly, "You look like you are turning grey in that job!" In her heart, Sarah knew it was true. "Sarah, what will happen if you stay on the job and do nothing?" her friend asked? Sarah had pretty much played it safe her whole life and leaving her job was out of her comfort zone, yet the prospect of staying in this job made her ill—she couldn't answer the question. Sarah's friend confronted her, "What do you really want to do? Think about what you would do with your career if you knew you could not fail?"

This question was surprisingly easy to answer. Sarah wanted to work and grow in an area that she had gifting and passion for, and that was gardening. For Sarah, there was simply nothing like working outdoors in her garden. Gardening was like painting a picture for Sarah, starting with something that looked plain and transforming it into something beautiful. She was somehow able to look at a yard and intuitively transform it in her mind, enveloping the greater spaces and the home or buildings in the space, and creating a design of native and natural plants in flowing patterns that blended into the environment. This is what she did. Sarah always had patience to get through the hard parts of a gardening project so that in the end she could look back at the beauty and say "WOW! I did this!"

Sarah had no formal training in landscaping or garden design, but she had shelves of books on gardening and landscape design from floor to ceiling in her living room. She was well read and known and respected for her expertise. Others called her for help; even those who had garden design credentials called her for advice. She clearly had a natural talent and great instincts that were obvious in her own beautiful landscaped yard and custom-designed gardens as well as in the work she had done for others.

Still, Sarah was reluctant to leave her job. It took a significant amount of courage for Sarah to take the necessary steps, but within six months she left her secure employment and began to live out her passion for gardening and her love of the outdoors. She started her own garden landscape and design company.

Sarah's business got off to a great start. Word of mouth about her landscape business spread quickly. Within a year she had more customers than she could handle. Sarah began employing people who were out of work and others from the community center who were homeless. She had a tremendous heart for those less fortunate, and as she mentored and encouraged her newly formed team, she found many of them proved to be dedicated and quite talented. Sarah felt this aspect of the business was an extra bonus!

Business continued to grow, and she became known in the community as a landmark employer of the unemployed and the homeless. Sarah was surprised and honored when the City Council recognized her as small businesswoman of the year and formally acknowledged her for her leadership in employing the people of the community.

Despite her success, four years into her venture she found herself struggling once again. The commitment and spark that energized her had dimmed. She was feeling extreme stress and found herself putting off her customers. The headaches and the negative stress she felt in her previous job had returned, and she wasn't sure she could continue the business. Sarah grew concerned about her future. Sarah's friend recommended that she call a coach.

Sarah called me and asked if I could come to her home for our first session; she wanted to give me a tour of her gardens. Her yard was a picture out of *Better Homes and Gardens;* her individual garden plots and perfect landscaping gave me a feeling of being someplace special. We finished the tour and went inside. Sarah explained why she had called me. She knew in her heart of hearts she wanted her business to thrive. There was nothing she was more passionate about than designing gardens, and they were indeed beautiful. Sarah knew she had been living out her dream. She loved to beautify her community and the surrounding areas with her work, and she was proud of the contribution her business was able to make to the community by employing those less fortunate. All these people had helped her realize her dream and now they counted on her for work. Still, she felt herself disengage, and things were taking a turn for the worse; little by little she felt herself withdrawing almost subconsciously.

Sarah said, "I want this business to be successful, but it's not working like I had hoped it would. I feel constant pressure with all the calls from customers and inquiries from potential customers. You'd think I'd be happy about it, yet I find myself not answering the calls. I will put my customers off for days at a time. They call back, each time more demanding." She paused for a moment, and sighed. "When I come in from a job at the end of a day and the phone starts to ring, it's just too much. I know I should answer, but I don't have the energy. I feel sick about it, but rather than call back, I avoid the customer altogether, and then later I feel guilty."

Sarah told lots of stories of unreasonable customers who she felt were difficult to deal with. As much as I tried to redirect with my questions, she kept going back to the same thing: her frustration with her customers, a sense of dissatisfaction, and unreasonable expectations that she felt were being put on her.

She made it clear that she did not want to close down her business and quit, but her feelings were getting in the way of doing the good job she had once done. I made a note that her vision was to maintain a successful business.

I was sensing the struggle between the customer demands on her time and the time she needed for herself after a full day's work. I asked some clarifying questions, "Sarah, what is this telling you?"

"I don't have normal business hours," Sarah answered with another sigh. "I get calls sometimes until 10 o'clock at night and all weekend long. It's crazy!" she said raising her voice. "And it's not just the calls, it's also the expectation that I fix a problem or bid a job immediately. It's unreasonable, so I just tune it out!"

Then Sarah admitted, "I know this has impacted my business. Customers are turning away because I'm not being responsive. Each month, I've seen the receivables decline."

I watched as she shrunk down in her chair and looked down at the floor.

As we continued, I began to see a polarity emerge, a polarity of Focusing on Customers and Focusing on Self. I was seeing her on the downside of Focusing on Customers, and Early Warnings that included not returning her customers' calls and sabotaging herself, which was impacting her bottom line.

Name the Poles

I followed my intuition and began to outline a Polarity Map. Sarah saw what I was drawing and asked about it. I gave Sarah a brief overview of Polarity Management and I talked about what could be learned by using the map. I felt that we needed to uncover the values and fears that she held around this polarity, and I knew that by using a Polarity Map we could bring clarity to what the issues really were. With that brief explanation, I shared what I thought was creating the tension in her life—a tension between Focusing on Customers and Focusing on Self. This sparked Sarah's curiosity and she wanted to know more. I asked Sarah if she wanted to coach using the Polarity Map. She agreed. I drew out a map and we looked at it together.

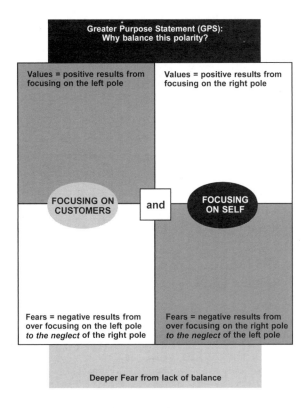

Polarity Map #1

I asked her to relax in her chair and told her that I would ask the questions and work through the map. Sarah sat back and we began.

Starting from the top left of the Polarity Map, I started with the values she held of focusing on her customers by asking, "Sarah, take me to a time when you were out there engaging with your customers and it was going really well. What was working at that time? What made it work?"

Sarah relaxed deeper into her chair, and as she reflected, a smile came to her face. "I loved interacting with my customers and discussing their projects, and it was so great to see the look on my customers' faces when I shared my ideas.

Upper Left Quadrant for Focusing on Customers

I really loved that. My business was growing by word of mouth, so I didn't have to advertise—my advertisement was a job well done. My own financial situation was going better than I had ever imagined, and I didn't have to worry about paying my bills."

As Sarah talked, I began filling in the upside of Focusing on Customers. Her eyes sparkled as she continued, "The business was growing, and there was too much for me to do myself. That was great because I was able to employ people who really needed a job, and they were so grateful for the work. I taught them to read my blueprints, and they did an excellent job; many were really interested and they worked hard. I was outside a good share of the day with my crew, getting lots of physical exercise and feeling great. It was just a great feeling to take care of my customers and help those less fortunate."

I could feel Sarah's excitement and passion as she spoke. "Sarah, I can feel your enthusiasm and your joy," I said.

"Oh yes, I can't really explain it—it was just the best time of my life," Sarah said thinking back.

Sarah had given me a lot of information, and I completed my notes on the values quadrant of Focusing on Customers.

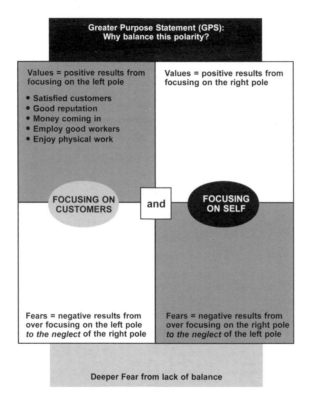

Polarity Map #2

Looking straight into her eyes, I began again, "Sarah, tell me about what happened next; what changed?"

Sarah's smile left her face as she began, "Once my business started taking off, I knew I'd be working long days and I felt up for the challenge. I'd be out in the field during the day and spend nights and weekends placing orders, scheduling deliveries, dealing with customers, and working the books. But now working day and night has become too much—I can't keep up that pace. If I really want to take care of my customers, I have to be on the job during the day and answer phone calls and e-mail at night and on weekends." Sarah said with a tense look on her face, "I feel drained; I don't have enough time or the energy for all the work, let alone anything else for me. I'm burned out, and I'm not enjoying my business as I once did. I have begun to resent my customers for demanding so much of me. I fear that my dream has become a nightmare."

> **Lower Left Quadrant for Focusing on Customers**

Those were strong words. It was clear to me Sarah's difficulties and complaints about her customers came from experiencing her fears, and even while in the downside of Focusing on Customers, she felt she had to "hang in there" through the stress, staying focused on the tasks at hand. I filled in the second quadrant, and made note that her dream had become a nightmare.

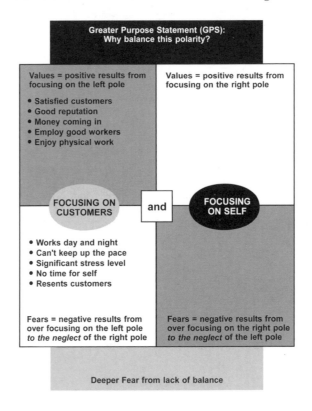

Polarity Map #3

Shifting toward Focusing on Self, I asked, "What do you want for yourself that you don't have now, Sarah?"

"I can't come home every night to phone calls and paper work—I can't do it!" she said firmly. "I want better time management so that I don't have to work late into the night and all

> **Upper-Right Quadrant for Caring for Self**

weekend long. What I want is to work outdoors—I love gardening and land-scaping, so I know this is my passion, but I need to manage my time better and eliminate some stress. Maybe I need some help with that. When I started my business, I wasn't in the field every day all day, so I had time to work through my e-mails and return phone calls on my slower days, and I tried to keep Sunday as a day for myself—my day off. That's what I want. I want to look forward to talking with my customers, and I want to maintain a good rapport. What I really want for myself is to live my dream!" Sarah said from deep within herself.

Pausing a moment to let the intensity of her desires settle in, I jotted my notes in the upper right quadrant of Focusing on Self. I also noted the Greater Purpose Statement as it seemed clear

Greater Purpose and Deeper Fear

to me now that Sarah's Greater Purpose was to live her dream, and checking my notes I saw "Dream had become nightmare," which I wrote in as the Deeper Fear.

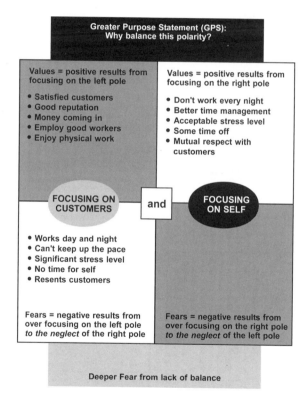

Polarity Map #4

Looking at the sketch of the Polarity Map and the downside of Focusing on Self, I asked, "So tell me, Sarah, what happens when you focus on yourself to the neglect of customers?"

Sarah didn't really understand what I was asking.

I explained, "No matter how much you want to focus on your customers and spend your time focusing on your customers, at some point, you can't neglect yourself any longer, and you must

> **Lower Right Quadrant for Focusing on Self**

stop and focus on yourself. But what if you only focused on yourself and simply neglected your customers?"

Sarah understood. She said matter of factly, "My customers would be dissatisfied."

"Good. What else?" I asked.

"Well, without satisfied customers, my reputation would suffer. That would mean no new word-of-mouth customers, and the customers I have would probably decide to work with someone else next time, because they wouldn't be getting the attention they were paying for."

"What else?" I asked continuing to drill down.

"So, my business would dry up and I wouldn't have work for myself or the workers I employ, and obviously that would not be good!" Sarah responded.

"And what would that mean?" I asked again.

"I wouldn't be living out my passion," Sarah confessed as her voice wound down.

I finished filling in the map with my final notes.

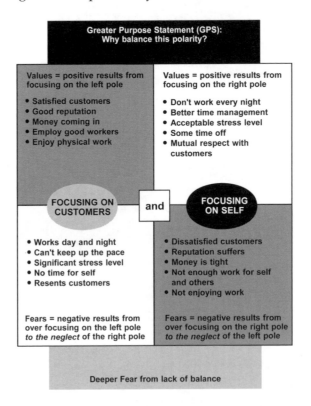

Polarity Map #5

"Sarah, I know you hired a coach to help solve a problem," I went on. "I don't think we have a problem to solve. I think we have a polarity to manage."

With a puzzled look, Sarah said, "I'm not sure I understand."

"I'd like to show you what I mean," I said. "Let me get something out of the car." I returned with easel pad, painter's tape, and markers.

Using tape, I broke her living room floor into the four quadrants of a Polarity Map. I rewrote the notes from each quadrant of my handwritten paper onto individual sheets of easel paper, and then I laid each piece of easel paper on the floor into its proper quadrant. I added the polarity of Focusing on Customers and Focusing on Self, the Greater Purpose, Deeper Fear, and at the top of the map I added the vision statement I heard her coming back to time-and-time again, Maintaining a Successful Business.

When I had arranged all the pieces, Sarah and I stood at the base of the map and looked at the entire picture.

Maintaining a Successful Business

Greater Purpose Statement (GPS): Why balance this polarity?	
Values = positive results from focusing on the left pole • Satisfied customers • Good reputation • Money coming in • Employ good workers • Enjoy physical work	Values = positive results from focusing on the right pole • Don't work every night • Better time management • Acceptable stress level • Some time off • Mutual respect with customers
FOCUSING ON CUSTOMERS and	**FOCUSING ON SELF**
• Works day and night • Can't keep up the pace • Significant stress level • No time for self • Resents customers	• Dissatisfied customers • Reputation suffers • Money is tight • Not enough work for self and others • Not enjoying work
Fears = negative results from over focusing on the left pole *to the neglect* of the right pole	Fears = negative results from over focusing on the right pole *to the neglect* of the left pole
Deeper Fear from lack of balance	

Polarity Map #6

"Wow," she said, "what's all this?"

"It's a Polarity Map. Let's walk through it," I said.

Sarah nodded in agreement, "Okay," she said.

Pointing to the vision statement, I said, "First, I heard you say several times and in different ways that you really want to maintain a successful business."

Sarah nodded her head to affirm.

"And I am hearing that you want to live out that dream," I said pointing to the rectangle on top of the Polarity Map, then shifting our attention to the rectangle on the bottom of the Polarity Map, I added, "and that your Deeper Fear is that your dream will become a nightmare."

Sarah's body seemed to shrink as she nodded in agreement again.

"I'm also hearing the tension lies between focusing on your customers and focusing on yourself. The tension around focusing on customers and focusing on yourself tells me that these are an 'interdependent pair,' a pair dependent on one another."

"Okay," Sarah said as she nodded slowly to show some understanding. "Can I change the interdependent pair?" she asked.

"Yes, absolutely," I said earnestly, "this is your map."

"I think the tension lies between finding time to care for my customers and time to care for myself," Sarah said slowly. "The words 'care for' really resonate with me. I really do care for my customers, and I really do need to care for myself."

I changed the polarity of Focus on Customers and Focus on Self to Caring for Customers and Caring for Self.

Renaming the Poles

Then I asked Sarah to stand with me in the upside of Caring for Customers. As we looked down at the words in this quadrant I continued, "This is where you were the first few years of your business. You attracted customers, your reputation spread by word of mouth, you were making the money you wanted to make, you were even able to employ others, and you enjoyed the physical aspects of your work." We stood together in the upside of the values quadrant of Caring for Customers as Sarah looked down at the map and she re-read the words.

"Yes," she acknowledged. "This was my dream and I was living out my dream!" she echoed softly.

"Now something has changed," I said, as together we moved to stand in the downside quadrant of Caring for Customers. "Your dream became so real and so successful that after working all day in the field, you come home to e-mails and phone calls, and all this has begun to spill over into your weekends." Now you don't feel you can keep up the challenging pace, and you are experiencing significant stress."

As I read through the downside of Caring for Customers, I could sense Sarah's body language tighten up, and I saw tension come into her face.

I continued, "You have no time for yourself, and you are finding yourself resenting your customers, putting them off, or ignoring them."

After a pause, Sarah spoke slowly and softly, "That's where I am right now."

Staring down at the words on the map, Sarah continued. "I'm moving toward my Deeper Fear and my dream is becoming a nightmare! How did I get here?" she asked holding her hands together and pressing them to her heart.

This seemed like the perfect time to draw in an Infinity Loop to show the natural movement from the present problem state to the preferred future state. I took out a marker and drew an Infinity Loop across the map.

Maintaining a Successful Business

Greater Purpose Statement (GPS): Why balance this polarity? LIVE OUT MY DREAM	
Values = positive results from focusing on the left pole	Values = positive results from focusing on the right pole
• Satisfied customers • Good reputation • Money coming in • Employ good workers • Enjoy physical work	• Don't work every night • Better time management • Acceptable stress level • Some time off • Mutual respect with customers
CARING FOR CUSTOMERS **and**	CARING FOR SELF
• Works day and night • Can't keep up the pace • Significant stress level • No time for self • Resents customers	• Dissatisfied customers • Reputation suffers • Money is tight • Not enough work for self and others • Not enjoying work
Fears = negative results from over focusing on the left pole *to the neglect* of the right pole	Fears = negative results from over focusing on the right pole *to the neglect* of the left pole
DREAM BECOMES A NIGHTMARE Deeper Fear from lack of balance	

Polarity Map #7

"You see, Sarah, because Caring for Customers and Caring for Self are interdependent pairs—when you over focus on Caring for Customers to the neglect of Caring for Self—you will eventually find yourself in the downside of Caring for Customers. It's not intentional; it is the inherent nature of how a polarity works. You follow the Infinity Loop because you

> **Infinity Loop**

can't maintain an over focus on your customers to the neglect of caring for yourself," I explained.

"Okay, I think I understand," as some of the anxiety left her voice. "So what happens next?" Sarah asked cautiously.

"Let's follow the Infinity Loop and see," I encouraged as we stepped into the values quadrant, or upside of Focusing on Self. Sarah's hands relaxed to her side.

I began gently, yet firmly. "When you are here, you are in the upside of Caring for Self. Here you focus on managing your time in a way that works for you. Managing your work time reduces your stress, and by incorporating some time off, you are rested and refreshed and better able to deal with customers, which fosters mutual respect."

"I get this!" Sarah said smiling, "I hadn't thought about caring for myself as being related to my business and my ability to care for my customers in that way before. Now I can see how connected they really are." She explained, "When I worked in the government office and left work for the day to come home, home was home. It was easier to have separate time to care for myself. I would decide to go do something with my friends, or stay home and read; it was my time and I managed it. Now when I come home, home is work. I want to take care of myself and do something for me, and then the phone rings and I have to answer it because it's a customer. But I'm irritated about it. I have no time to care for myself."

"Yes!" I agreed. "And now let's see if the next quadrant fits."

We moved into the downside of Caring for Self.

Sarah started, "So when I'm planning to take care of myself, I get upset when the telephone rings. I'm irritated with my customers, and I don't want to deal with them, so sometimes I don't answer the phone. They keep calling and I get even more irritated, and when we do finally talk, I don't treat them very well. I know word travels quickly, and when my customer tells others how they were treated, my reputation suffers. Of course, what follows is less business, which means less money, and I won't have the cash flow to keep people employed. The end result is all the joy is gone, and the dream has become a nightmare—YUK!"

Sarah continued to look at the map we had laid out on the floor. "I don't want my dream to become a nightmare," she said firmly. "I want to be better to my customers, and I want to be better to myself. I want both!"

"This is where Action Steps and Early Warnings come in," I said.

I went to the easel pad and drew Action Steps and Early Warning charts and laid them next to the Polarity Map.

Maintaining a Successful Business

Action Steps	Greater Purpose Statement (GPS): Why balance this polarity? LIVE OUT MY DREAM	Action Steps
How will we gain or maintain the positive results from focusing on this left pole? What? Who? By when? Measures?		How will we gain or maintain the positive results from focusing on this right pole? What? Who? By when? Measures?

Values = positive results from focusing on the left pole

- Satisfied customers
- Good reputation
- Money coming in
- Employ good workers
- Enjoy physical work

Values = positive results from focusing on the right pole

- Don't work every night
- Better time management
- Acceptable stress level
- Some time off
- Mutual respect with customers

CARING FOR CUSTOMERS **and** CARING FOR SELF

Early Warnings

Measurable indicators (things you can count) that will let you know that you are getting into the downside of this left pole.

- Works day and night
- Can't keep up the pace
- Significant stress level
- No time for self
- Resents customers

- Dissatisfied customers
- Reputation suffers
- Money is tight
- Not enough work for self and others
- Not enjoying work

Early Warnings

Measurable indicators (things you can count) that will let you know that you are getting into the downside of this right pole.

Fears = negative results from over focusing on the left pole *to the neglect* of the right pole

Fears = negative results from over focusing on the right pole *to the neglect* of the left pole

DREAM BECOMES A NIGHTMARE

Deeper Fear from lack of balance

Polarity Map #8

I explained that the objective is to get the best of both upsides, focusing on and spiraling up toward the Greater Purpose, and I drew in the Virtuous Cycle. I explained how Action Steps are used as a way to maintain the Greater Purpose of living out ones dream. They are measurable and provide a basis for accountability and self-correction.

Virtuous Cycle

Then I described how Early Warnings are indicators that allow you to anticipate and respond to the downside experiences of each pole. Action Steps are then taken in response to Early Warnings of the other interdependent pole to keep from spiraling down toward the Deeper Fear, and I illustrated this as I drew in the Vicious Cycle. I explained that acknowledging Early Warnings quickly and responding with Action Steps keeps the infinity loop in the upside of the two poles and moving toward the Greater Purpose.

Vicious Cycle

Maintaining a Successful Business

Action Steps

How will we gain or maintain the positive results from focusing on this left pole? What? Who? By when? Measures?

Greater Purpose Statement (GPS):
Why balance this polarity?
LIVE OUT MY DREAM

Values = positive results from focusing on the left pole

- Satisfied customers
- Good reputation
- Money coming in
- Employ good workers
- Enjoy physical work

Values = positive results from focusing on the right pole

- Don't work every night
- Better time management
- Acceptable stress level
- Some time off
- Mutual respect with customers

Action Steps

How will we gain or maintain the positive results from focusing on this right pole? What? Who? By when? Measures?

CARING FOR CUSTOMERS and **CARING FOR SELF**

Early Warnings

Measurable indicators (things you can count) that will let you know that you are getting into the downside of this left pole.

- Works day and night
- Can't keep up the pace
- Significant stress level
- No time for self
- Resents customers

- Dissatisfied customers
- Reputation suffers
- Money is tight
- Not enough work for self and others
- Not enjoying work

Early Warnings

Measurable indicators (things you can count) that will let you know that you are getting into the downside of this right pole.

Fears = negative results from over focusing on the left pole *to the neglect* of the right pole

Fears = negative results from over focusing on the right pole *to the neglect* of the left pole

DREAM BECOMES A NIGHTMARE

Deeper Fear from lack of balance

Polarity Map #9

"Where would you like to start?" I asked Sarah.

Still a little unsure of how Action Steps and Early Warnings worked, Sarah said, "I get that I can't really take care of my customers until I take care of myself, so let's start with the Action Steps I need to do that."

As we looked back up to the values identified in the upside of Caring for Self, I said, "Okay, let's look again at the upside of Caring for Self, and tell me what Action Steps you can take that will hold you accountable to maintaining those values."

Sarah began with managing her time in her office. She decided that to make this work, she would need some help. "I may have to hire someone for a few hours a week to do my ordering, work the accounts payable, and maybe do the payroll—maybe even answer some phone calls and take messages. I

Action Steps to refocus on Caring for Self

know it's a bit of a risk right now in terms of adding staff, but if I want to maintain a successful business, it's a risk I need to take. I think having someone even 10 or 15 hours a week would help me manage my office better and reduce my stress."

I took notes as Sarah continued. "I have had very little time off since starting this business four years ago, and caring for myself means Sundays to myself, to do what I want to do."

I wrote "Sundays off."

Sarah continued, "I really want to have better relationships with my customers, so I'll have to put something in place to accomplish that."

As a polarity coach, I could see this as either a Caring for Customer Action Step or a Caring for Self Action Step; it is true that taking care of the customer is taking care of self and the reverse.

I cautioned her, "Sarah, I want to make sure you feel that this is about caring for you and not about caring for your customers."

Sarah assured me that it definitely made her feel better to have good rapport with her customers, that it would alleviate her personal stress just to know communication with her customers was going smoothly, and that there was mutual respect. She felt this really was about taking control and managing her time, which would help her take care of herself.

"I would like to respond in a better way to my customers' calls, so I need to keep that in mind," Sarah said. "My goal should be to return calls within 24 hours, if not sooner. I'd also like to make proactive contact by checking in with them every so often." Sarah said firmly, "I'd like to find time to call one of my customers each week just to check in, or maybe stop by to chat for a few minutes if I'm in the area. I'd really enjoy that."

I finished writing in the Action Steps for Caring for Self.

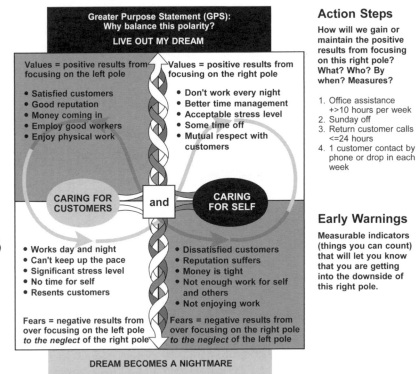

Polarity Map #10

Sarah seemed satisfied with those Action Steps.

"What's next?" I asked.

"Let's follow the Infinity Loop to the downside of Caring for Self and try some Early Warnings," Sarah answered.

"Great!" I said in agreement. "What measurable indicators would let you know you are over focusing on Caring for Self to the neglect of customers?"

"Oh, that's easy," Sarah answered quickly. "If I were neglecting my customers, eventually I'd lose my customers; word of mouth would be negative rather than positive, so new customers would be hard to come by."

As I made these notes, I questioned, "Okay, what else?"

Pausing for a moment, Sarah thought, "I think an early warning would be having fewer than three jobs in the pipeline. If that happens, I know money will get tight and within a month or so there would be a lull. I

> **Early Warnings due to an over focus on Caring for Self**

might be tempted to look the other way and take some time off when I really should be drumming up business."

"That makes a lot of sense," I said affirming Sarah's understanding of herself and her business needs.

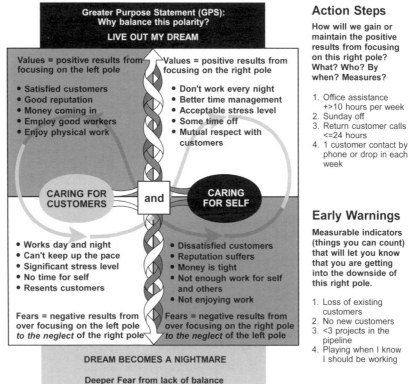

Polarity Map #11

"Okay, so moving from what you don't want, the downside of Caring for Self, toward what you do want, the upside of Caring for Customers, what things are you already doing and what else could you do in order to take care of your customers?" I asked.

"I want to see that look of satisfaction on my customers' faces once again, and continue to grow the business by word of mouth," Sarah said.

Action Steps to refocus on Caring for Customers

"How do you really know they are satisfied?" I asked.

Sarah thought, "I guess I don't know for sure, other than my instincts have been right in the past. Still, I have been thinking of putting a little survey together and using that information to better gauge customer satisfaction."

"Great idea," I affirmed, "and what about word of mouth? How will you know this is happening? Can you put a number on it?"

"I don't advertise, so I would say if I am asked to bid on five or more jobs a month and if I am winning at least three of those jobs," Sarah clarified, "this would be enough to manage the cash flow. I could continue to employ my workers," she said, pointing to her value of keeping others employed. "I would not have predicted this, but employing those less fortunate has become a very important part of living my dream."

"Anything else?" I asked.

Sarah thought, "I guess the final piece is to limit my time in the field to four days a week. I could spend all my time working the job sites, but I should begin to assign some lead workers oversight responsibility so that I can spend some time in the office during the weekday. Four days in the field will be enough to oversee the jobs and satisfy my love of the out of doors, plus, I know cutting back will help me stay on the upside and not over focus on my customers.

Maintaining a Successful Business

Action Steps		Action Steps
How will we gain or maintain the positive results from focusing on this left pole? What? Who? By when? Measures?	**Greater Purpose Statement (GPS): Why balance this polarity?** **LIVE OUT MY DREAM**	How will we gain or maintain the positive results from focusing on this right pole? What? Who? By when? Measures?
	Values = positive results from focusing on the left pole / Values = positive results from focusing on the right pole	
1. Customer survey results 2. Bid 5 jobs per month 3. Win 3 jobs per month 4. Worksite 4 days per week	• Satisfied customers • Good reputation • Money coming in • Employ good workers • Enjoy physical work / • Don't work every night • Better time management • Acceptable stress level • Some time off • Mutual respect with customers	1. Office assistance +>10 hours per week 2. Sunday off 3. Return customer calls <=24 hours 4. 1 customer contact by phone or drop in each week
	CARING FOR CUSTOMERS and **CARING FOR SELF**	
Early Warnings		**Early Warnings**
Measurable indicators (things you can count) that will let you know that you are getting into the downside of this left pole.	• Works day and night • Can't keep up the pace • Significant stress level • No time for self • Resents customers / • Dissatisfied customers • Reputation suffers • Money is tight • Not enough work for self and others • Not enjoying work	Measurable indicators (things you can count) that will let you know that you are getting into the downside of this right pole.
	Fears = negative results from over focusing on the left pole *to the neglect of the right pole* / Fears = negative results from over focusing on the right pole *to the neglect of the left pole*	1. Loss of existing customers 2. No new customers 3. <3 projects in the pipeline 4. Playing when I know I should be working
	DREAM BECOMES A NIGHTMARE Deeper Fear from lack of balance	

Polarity Map #12

Sarah was really beginning to understand how polarities work.

With one section yet to fill, we looked to the Early Warnings of over focus on Caring for Customers.

"Finally, Sarah, what will warn you that you are over focused on Caring for Customers?" I asked.

Sarah answered, "The Early Warnings could be spending every night and weekend in my office. I know I have to spend some nights and probably Saturdays working, but to stay on the upside of Caring for Customers, I will stay no more than four nights a week and no more than two hours each night, and I'd like to claim Sundays and at least one Saturday a month for myself.

Early Warnings due to an over focus on Caring for Customers

"Are you sure that is workable?" I asked.

"Yes, I've been spending a lot more time than that, but if I hire an office assistant and free myself from being on the job site every day, I believe this is doable."

"Anything else?" I asked.

"Yes, there is one more thing. When I begin to feel like I'm feeling stressed and I'm not enjoying myself, I know I can become terse with my customers, or find myself feeling too pressured. That's when I have to ask for help, take a day off, and then get back at it," Sarah concluded.

"Anything else?" I asked again.

"I think that's it," she said. "If I manage my time well, I think I will also be able to manage my stress. I've built in time for myself, and if I'm intentional about that, I'll feel more refreshed and better able to deal with those demanding phone calls," Sarah noted as we looked at the map.

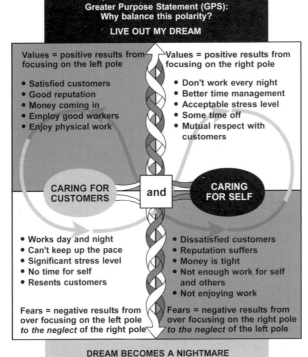

Polarity Map #13

I noticed that Sarah had gotten very quiet. Turning to look at her, I saw that she was crying.

"Why the tears?" I asked gently.

"It's so clear to me now," she said. "This is the garden of my life. The Early Warning signs are the weeds, and that is where I need to do my weeding, and the Action Steps are where I have to plant seeds. And when I plant the seeds, I know that I'm going to see flowers. It's not going to happen overnight, but eventually those flowers will bloom, and I can maintain a successful business. I can live out my dream!" Sarah said with confidence.

As I got into my car to leave, I was truly excited for Sarah, as she would be able to begin again with her business, and this time know how caring for herself was equally as important as caring for her customers; this time she had the whole picture.

Later Sarah told me she had redrawn the map on a flip chart and hung it over her computer. She would look at it every single day and make little pencil notes and additions to it with things she hadn't thought of that first day of coaching. She told me weeks later that her Polarity Map helped her transform the way she looked at her business. It gave her a sense of control about things so that she could draw a clearer line between herself and her customers. Sarah knew that managing her polarity well had begun to improve her business and bring balance to her life.

~

It is true that we often approach difficulties as problems to solve. Unfortunately, as Sarah learned, when we do this, we are only working on half the problem. Most often we see obstacles rather than patterns, and we back away from the issue seeing only the negative, rather than to move forward and embrace a full set of values. Polarity Coaching helped Sarah uncover the pattern, see the polarity that she needed to manage, identify her values, and take Action Steps toward her Greater Purpose.

Conclusion

Polarity Management® applies science and structure to supplement and balance the art and skill of a coaching conversation. As coaches begin to recognize polarities and introduce polarities to their clients, they will come to understand the significant potential of blending coaching and Polarity Management®. Coaches and clients alike will see how this simple, yet powerful tool can make a difference in breaking down barriers, identifying solutions, and developing strategies that result in effective action steps as they work to achieve their goals and visions.

Many really good books have been written about coaching and coaching techniques; I hope you have found that this book is one of them.

> "The test of a first-rate intelligence is the ability to hold two opposed ideas in mind at the same time and still retain the ability to function."
>
> – F. Scott Fitzgerald

Appendix A
Polarities to Manage

Work	and	Home
Caring for self	and	Caring for others
Planned	and	Spontaneous
Activity	and	Rest
Directive	and	Participative
Gentle love	and	Tough love
Caring for customers	and	Caring for self
Flexible	and	Rigid
Creating	and	Status quo
Critical analysis	and	Encouragement
Debate	and	Action
Stability	and	Change
Retain employees	and	Hire new talent
Feeling	and	Speaking
Equality	and	Uniqueness
Doing	and	Being
Connected	and	Separated
Responsibility	and	Freedom
Reflection	and	Action
Emotional	and	Physical
Fun through openness	and	Fun through accomplishment
New choices	and	Refined choices
Breakthrough ideas	and	Usable ideas
Slow	and	Speed
New choices	and	Refined choices

Breakthrough ideas	and	Usable ideas
Slow	and	Speed
Support	and	Evaluation
Mission	and	Margin
Frankness	and	Diplomacy
Exclusion	and	Inclusion
Diversity	and	Alignment
Connectedness	and	Uniqueness
Style	and	Substance
Exclusion	and	Inclusion
Diversity	and	Alignment
Connectedness	and	Uniqueness
Style	and	Substance
Bliss	and	Survival
Give	and	Receive
Be focused	and	Hand loose
Grounded	and	Busy
Be sure in self	and	Be vulnerable
Grab on	and	Let go
Stop, listen, learn	and	Speak up
Use what I know	and	Learn new
Push	and	Pull
Quiet	and	Loud
Work for money	and	Work for joy
Stable	and	Fluid
Competitive	and	Collaborative
Power at grass roots	and	Power at the top
Care of organization	and	Care of customer
Globalization	and	Localization
Law	and	Grace
Head	and	Heart
Treasures	and	Trash

Strategic	and	Tactical
Over-caring	and	Divisive
Independence	and	Dependence
Individual	and	Community
Think as individual	and	Abilene Paradox
Fact	and	Fiction
Open	and	Closed
Lose	and	Gain
External	and	Internal
Happiness	and	Trials
Sorrow	and	Hope
Compassionate	and	Bold
Recognize the individual	and	Recognize the team
Care for my part of the organization	and	Care for the whole organization
Taking care of the organization	and	Taking care of the client
Centralized coordination	and	Decentralized focus
Profitability	and	Responsibility
Cost	and	Quality
Get the job done	and	Build relationships
Control	and	Surrender
Resting	and	Working
Clarity	and	Ambiguity
Control	and	Empowerment
Convergent	and	Divergent
Constraint	and	Chaos
Compliance	and	Choice
Past/present	and	Future
Inhaling	and	Exhaling
Self	and	Other
Part	and	Whole
Individual	and	Team

Separate	and	Connected
Stability	and	Change
Centralized coordination	and	Decentralized focus
Cost	and	Quality
Get the job done	and	Build relationships
Traditionalist	and	Change agent
Practical application	and	Theoretical understanding
Thoroughness (depth)	and	Efficiency (breadth)
Tight	and	Loose
Long term	and	Short term
Plan for your future	and	Be in your future
Feminine	and	Masculine
Unify	and	Debate
Evolutionary	and	Revolutionary
Mandatory	and	Discretionary
Confidence	and	Humility
Grounded	and	Visionary
Logic	and	Creativity
Vengeance	and	Atonement
Planning	and	Implementing
Differences	and	Commonalities
Poised	and	Clumsy
Celebrate every person	and	Celebrate based on performance
Resistance	and	Surrender
Keep	and	Share
Develop	and	Align
Either/or	and	Both/and

Appendix B
Questions for Coaching Polarities

What's important here; what's not?

What should be amplified; what should be dampened?

What needs to be put on the shelf; what needs to be taken off the shelf?

What's important to start; what's important to finish?

What are the obvious differences; what are the obvious similarities?

What are the subtle differences; what are the subtle similarities?

What are the obvious differences; what differences are hard to see?

What is irritating; what is satisfying?

What was hard; what was easy?

When will you listen; when will you speak?

What's connected here; what appears disconnected?

What's your snap judgment telling you; what is your intentional judgment telling you?

What is the dominant theme; what is the underlying or insignificant theme?

What needs to be planned; what can be spontaneous?

What strengths were visible; how did your weaknesses show up?

In what way did you overreact; in what way did you underreact?

What should you contribute; what should you keep back?

What needs to be addressed; what can go by the wayside?

When would logic work best; when would a playful approach be best?

What are you suspicious of; what do you trust?

What do you need to think about; what do you need to say to others?

What will you engage in; what will you let go of?

What are you able to see; what are you able to feel?

What is vivid; what is vague?

Where is the conflict; where is the harmony?

What is agreed upon; what is in disagreement?

What can you control; what is outside of your control?

What do you want to keep; what do you want to throw away?

What are you comfortable with; what are you concerned about?

What would you include; what would you avoid?

What will you mourn; what will you celebrate?

What do you need to think about; what action should you take?

What can take it deeper; what can take it wider?

What brings you down; what do you thrive on?

What maximizes your energy; what minimizes your energy?

What brings you strength; what weakens you?

What's positive about this; what's negative about this?

What do you have to finish; what can you disregard?

What needs to be said; what can be left unsaid?

What's true here when you look at yourself; what's true when you look at others?

What about this is complex; what about this is simple?

What's acceptable here; what's unacceptable?

What can you do for yourself; what can you do for others?

What are you reluctant to do; what do you know you must do?

What do you know intuitively; what will you have to learn?

What needs to be said; what should be kept to yourself?

What is organized; what feels cluttered?

When do you focus on strengths; when do you focus on weaknesses?

When should you inject humor; when should you be serious?

What is natural; what is forced?

What are the facts saying; what does your intuition say?

What can you rely on; what are you unsure of?

What can you picture; what isn't clear?

What do others perceive; what do you perceive?

What sharpens your ideas; what dulls your thoughts?

What can you shift that will make a difference; what should stay the same?

When should you draw near; when should you back away?

What drives your emotion; what drives your logic?

What is the strongest link; what is the weakest link?

What is the truth; what is false?

What should be revealed now; what should be left alone?

Looking back, what do you see; what does the future hold?

About the Author

Kathy Anderson is a Polarity Coach, Organization Development Consultant, and Project Manager. She founded Freedom to Change, Coaching and Consulting in 2001 while attending the Coaches Training Institute (CTI) Co-Active Coaches Training program. Attending the Polarity Management® Consultant Development Intensive program in 2006 opened the door to blending these two disciplines in her coaching and consulting practice.

Kathy holds an MBA in Management and a Masters Certificate in Organization Development from St. Thomas University, and a Bachelor of Arts in Psychology from Metropolitan State University, Saint Paul, Minnesota; her professional experience spans 30 years in both the private and public sectors. Kathy is a Polarity Management® Associate and is a certified coach, having completed programs with the Lifeforming Leadership Coaching Institute and the Coaches Training Institute. Kathy also holds certification with the Human Systems Dynamics Institute. As a life-long learner, Kathy has logged thousands of classroom hours in human resource management, project management, process improvement, human dynamics, human services, and technical training.

Kathy and her husband, Bob, live in Saint Paul, Minnesota. This is Kathy's third book. Other books by the author are:

A Gift of Love: The Story of My Mother's Dying Time

and soon to be published,

Alex and Granny: A Children's Story of Intergenerational Love